T0185687

Communications
in Computer and Information Science   1672

Editorial Board Members

Joaquim Filipe ⓘ
   Polytechnic Institute of Setúbal, Setúbal, Portugal

Ashish Ghosh
   Indian Statistical Institute, Kolkata, India

Raquel Oliveira Prates ⓘ
   Federal University of Minas Gerais (UFMG), Belo Horizonte, Brazil

Lizhu Zhou
   Tsinghua University, Beijing, China

More information about this series at https://link.springer.com/bookseries/7899

Ritika Mehra · Phayung Meesad ·
Sateesh K. Peddoju · Dhajvir S. Rai (Eds.)

Computational Intelligence and Smart Communication

First International Conference, ICCISC 2022
Dehradun, India, June 10–11, 2022
Revised Selected Papers

Springer

Editors
Ritikà Mehra ⓘ
Dev Bhoomi Uttarakhand University
Dehradun, India

Phayung Meesad ⓘ
King Mongkut University of Technology
Bangkok, Thailand

Sateesh K. Peddoju ⓘ
Indian Institute of Technology Roorkee
Roorkee, India

Dhajvir S. Rai
College of Engineering Roorkee
Roorkee, India

ISSN 1865-0929 ISSN 1865-0937 (electronic)
Communications in Computer and Information Science
ISBN 978-3-031-22914-5 ISBN 978-3-031-22915-2 (eBook)
https://doi.org/10.1007/978-3-031-22915-2

© The Editor(s) (if applicable) and The Author(s), under exclusive license
to Springer Nature Switzerland AG 2022
This work is subject to copyright. All rights are reserved by the Publisher, whether the whole or part of the material is concerned, specifically the rights of translation, reprinting, reuse of illustrations, recitation, broadcasting, reproduction on microfilms or in any other physical way, and transmission or information storage and retrieval, electronic adaptation, computer software, or by similar or dissimilar methodology now known or hereafter developed.
The use of general descriptive names, registered names, trademarks, service marks, etc. in this publication does not imply, even in the absence of a specific statement, that such names are exempt from the relevant protective laws and regulations and therefore free for general use.
The publisher, the authors, and the editors are safe to assume that the advice and information in this book are believed to be true and accurate at the date of publication. Neither the publisher nor the authors or the editors give a warranty, expressed or implied, with respect to the material contained herein or for any errors or omissions that may have been made. The publisher remains neutral with regard to jurisdictional claims in published maps and institutional affiliations.

This Springer imprint is published by the registered company Springer Nature Switzerland AG
The registered company address is: Gewerbestrasse 11, 6330 Cham, Switzerland

Preface

A two-day International Conference on Computational Intelligence and Smart Communication (ICCISC 2022) was organized by the School of Computer Science and Engineering at Dev Bhoomi Uttarakhand University (DBUU), Dehradun, during June 10–11, 2022. This conference was organized in association with Springer. Our professional partners for this conference were the ACM Jaipur Chapter and the Dev Bhoomi Uttarakhand University CSI Student Chapter, and it was sponsored by the Uttarakhand State Council for Science & Technology and the Uttarakhand Science Education & Research Centre, Dehradun, India.

The aim of the conference was to provide a platform for researchers and practitioners from both academia and industry to meet and share cutting-edge developments in the field of computational intelligence and smart communication. It also focused on all aspects of computation intelligence and data sciences with modern and emerging computational topics.

ICCISC 2022 provided an excellent international forum to share knowledge as well as their findings in theory, methodology, and/or applications relevant to the conference themes. The conference featured paper presentations in addition to the keynote addresses from prominent speakers on related state-of-the-art technologies. The conference benefited the delegates by helping them to add to or improve their skills and knowledge. The networking during the conference also laid foundations for possible future collaborations. ICCISC 2022 provided an invaluable platform to raise awareness about forthcoming innovations in diverse fields of computational intelligence and smart communication.

The conference brought together a community of international researchers, industrial experts, and academicians. It not only was restricted to paper presentations but also paved the way for subsequent discussions on the latest trends in research and development linked to the conference themes and allied areas.

The conference featured keynote addresses by prominent people, including experts from the Cloud Lab at the University of Melbourne, Australia, the Artificial Intelligence Research Institute (IIIA-CSIC), Spain, the Multimedia Data Analytics and Processing Research Unit at Chulalongkorn University, Thailand, and the AI and Cybersecurity Research Centre at Staffordshire University, UK.

The main conference themes were as follows:

- Track 1: Wireless Sensor Networks and Computing Technologies
- Track 2: Networks, Security and Privacy
- Track 3: Smart Communication and Technology
- Track 4: Emerging Computing

Topics of interest included the following subthemes: block chain, deep learning, pattern recognition, modeling and simulation, natural language processing, internet of things, soft computing, artificial intelligence, quantum computing, cloud computing, fog computing, cyber security, sentiment analysis, wireless sensor networks, signal processing, intelligent communications and networking, software defined networks, 5G networks, mobile and optical broadband, e-health, real time networks, satellite and space communication, radar and microwaves, secure and energy efficient networks, cognitive radio and cognitive networks, multimedia communication, intelligent control, robotics, and smart embedded systems.

The review process is one of the major components that governs the quality of research being shared and the success of the event as well, thus making it a very critical part of a conference. To maintain transparency and to ensure that high standards and ethics of research are followed, the submission of papers was performed through the EasyChair conference management system. This platform has an included feature for plagiarism checks, which are performed using the Turnitin plagiarism software tool. Papers with a plagiarism coefficient of more than 30% plagiarism get rejected automatically. Papers with coefficients below 30% but above 12% were returned to the authors for revision. Papers having plagiarism coefficients below 12% in the literature review section (if any) were considered for presentation in conference provided they met other norms related to plagiarism.

A single-blind review process was followed, with each paper assigned to three independent reviewers. Most of the reviewers were external to ensure the quality standards of the conference. The process mandatorily required three reviews to be completed— no paper was considered for presentation unless all three reviews were received—and efforts were made to reassign papers in cases where a reviewer declined or expressed unavailability for the process. After receiving the reviews for a paper, it was judged on the basis of positive reviews and comments, and wherever applicable minor or major modifications as suggested by the reviewers were communicated to authors and the paper(s) revised as necessary.

If two or more reviews were found satisfactory, then only the paper was sent to the General Chair for further verification, and the acceptance or rejection of the paper was at the sole discretion of the General Chair, whilst keeping the reviewers' comments in mind. The conference received 106 papers from authors for consideration and, after the stringent review process, only 56 were shortlisted for presentation. Further, only nine research articles were considered for publication in Springer's CCIS series. Out of these nine, eight are full length papers and one is a short paper. We hope that you enjoy reading the selected papers.

October 2022

Ritika Mehra
Phayung Meesad
Sateesh K. Peddoju
Dhajvir S. Rai

Organization

General Chairs

Sanjay Bansal   Dev Bhoomi Uttarakhand University, India
Preety Kothiyal   Dev Bhoomi Uttarakhand University, India
Raj Kishore Tripathi   Dev Bhoomi Uttarakhand University, India

Program Committee Chairs

Ritika Mehra   Dev Bhoomi Uttarakhand University, India
Dhajvir Singh Rai   Dev Bhoomi Uttarakhand University, India

Steering Committee

Jean-Paul Van Belle   University of Cape Town, South Africa
Bhuvanesh Unhelkar   University of South Florida, USA
Ankit Agarwal   Northwestern University, USA
Phayung Meesad   King Mongkut's University of Technology, Thailand
Sateesh K. Peddoju   Indian Institute of Technology Roorkee, India
Waralak V. Siricharoen   Silpakorn University, Thailand
S. Gomathi   UK International Qualifications Limited, UK
R. C. Bansal   University of Sharjah, UAE
Michael Pecht   Maryland University, USA
Sachin R. Jain   Oklahoma State University, SUSA
Ahmed Elngar   Beni-Suef University, Egypt
Sanjeevi Padmanaban   Aalborg University, Esbjerg, Denmark
Ahmed J. Obaid   University of Kufa, Iraq
Balachandra Pattanaik   Wollega University, Ethiopia
Ali Musrrat   King Faisal University, Saudi Arabia
Mohammad Shoab   Shaqra University, Saudi Arabia
Rhonnel S. Paculanan   University of Makati, Philippines
Kourosh Ahmadi   Auckland Institute of Studies, New Zealand
Rocha Alvaro   University of Lisbon, Portugal
Pao Ann Hsuing   National Chung Cheng University, Taiwan
Durga Toshniwal   Indian Institute of Technology Roorkee, India
Kunwar Vaisla   Bipin Tripathi Kumauni Institute of Technology, India

Vishal Jain	Sharda University, India
Manoj Kumar Shukla	Harcourt Butler Technical University, India
Aman Jatin	Amity University, Gurgaun, India
Sandeep Vijay	Tula Institute, India
R. K. Bharti	Bipin Tripathi Kumaon Institute of Technology, India
Ajit Singh	Bipin Tripathi Kumaon Institute of Technology, India
Mayank Aggarwal	Gurukul Kangri Vishwavidyalaya, India
Amit Aggarwal	Abdul Kalam Institute of Technology, Tanakpur, India
Pramod Kumar	Krishna Engineering College, India
Vishal Kumar	Bipin Tripathi Kumauni Institute of Technology, India
S. C. Sharma	Indian Institute of Technology Roorkee, India
T. S. Arora	National Institute of Technology, India
Vibhash Yadav	REC Banda, India
Umesh Chandra	Banda University of Agriculture and Technology, India
Anish Gupta	Academy of Business and Engineering Science, India
Vaisla Kunwar	Bipin Tripathi Kumauni Institute of Technology, India
Sudhakar Chauhan	National Institute of Technology Kurukshetra, India
Kapil Gupta	National Institute of Technology Kurukshetra, India
Ved Prakash	Amity University, Haryana, India
Nilam Choudhary	Jaipur Engineering College and Research Centre, India
Baldev Singh	Vivekananda Global University, India
Suresh Kumar	Manav Rachna Institute of Research and Studies, India
Das Nripendra	Manipal University Jaipur, India
Vijay Bhaskar Semwal	Maulana Azad National Institute of Technology, India
Prakash S.	Bharath Institute of Higher Education and Research, India
Gaurav Verma	Jaypee Institute of Information Technology, India
Surya Prakash	Thapar University, India
R. Dhanasekaran	Syed Ammal Engineering College, India
M. K. Sharma	Amarpali Group of Institutions, India
Dinesh Goel	Poornima University, India

Parma Nand	Sharda University, India
Sachin Sharma	Graphic Era University, India

Program Committee

Diago Galar	Lulea University of Technology, Sweden
Omar H. Alhazmi	Taibah University, Saudi Arabia
Anand Nayyar	Duy Tan University, Vietnam
Pham Quoc Cuong	HCMUT-VNUHCM, Vietnam
Felix J. Garcia Clemente	University of Murcia, Spain
G. E. Alexender Cristina	Universidad Technica Particular de Loja, Ecuador
Sameeka Saini	Dev Bhoomi Uttarakhand University, India
Manik Sharma	DAV University, India
Jeetendra Pande	Uttarakhand Open University, India
Bagwari Ashish	WIT Dehradun, India
Gunjan Bhatnagar	Dev Bhoomi Uttarakhand University, India
Vivek Arya	Gurukul Kangri University, India
Vipul Sharma	Gurukul Kangri University, India
Bhawna Parihar	Bipin Tripathi Kumaon Institute of Technology, India
Poonam Chhimwal	Bipin Tripathi Kumaon Institute of Technology, India
Saurav Mishra	Dehradun Institute of Technology, India
Banit Negi	GBPIET, India
Alka Dikshit	Himachal Pradesh University, India
Ashish Nayar	IITM, India
Deepak Sharma	Jagan Institute of Management Studies Delhi, India
Jitendra Rauthan	GBPIET, India
Ekta Upadhayay	Dev Bhoomi Uttarakhand University, India
Varun Uniyal	GBPIET, India
Sunil Mankotiya	Himachal Pradesh University Shimla, India
Nishta Kapoor	Rajeev Gandhi Government Degree College Shimla, India
Anurag Jain	University of Petroleum and Energy Studies, India
Shamik Tiwari	University of Petroleum and Energy Studies, India
Pooja Munjal	Delhi University, India
Deepesh Rawat	SRHU Dehradun, India
K. C. Mishra	WIT Dehradun, India
Ajit Rathor	Ajay Kumar Garg Engineering College, India
Anuj Sharma	Gurukul Kangri University, India
Anupama Mishra	Swami Rama Himalayan University, India
D. C. Pandey	Graphic Era University, India

Vivek Kumar Gupta   Dehradun Institute of Technology, India
Vijay Shankar Sharma   Manipal University, India
Nemi Chand Barwar   Mugneeram Bangur Memorial Engineering
                           College, India

Additional Reviewers

Mukesh Joshi
Anvesha Katti
Purnendu Bikash Acharjee
Rajeev Kumar
Akhilesh Kumar Sharma
Gaurav Verma
Sandeep Budhani
Kapil Joshi
Gaurav Aggarwal
Anuj Kumar
Shilpa Srivastava
Aruna Pavate
Kanchan Dabre
Vaibhav Ranjan
Anupama Chadha
Ram Narayan
Sunil Kumar
Wiqas Ghai
Amit Kishor
Samya Muhuri
Atul Garg
Abhineet Anand
Mandeep Kaur
Nishant Mathur
Ahmed A. Thabit
Sanjeev Pippal
Madhulika Mittal
Vivek Arya
Jitendra Saturwar
Avdhesh Kumar Tiwari
Pooja Gupta
Gesu Thakur
Ashish Gupta
Sapana Singh
Bharti Sharma
Sridhar Iyer
Abhilasha Chauhan

Deepesh Rawat
Sateesh Kumar
Apurva Sharma
Anirudh Mangore
Pratap Singh
Ganesh Yadav
Shalini Puri
Bhagyashree Shendkar
Vineet Kumar Salar
Michael Albino
Sohit Agarwal
Naveen Tewari
Gaurav Goel
Ajesh F.
Vivek Sharma
Sonika Singh
Rajiv Kumar
Pronab Adhikari
Jefferson Costales
Rajat Goel
Rakesh Saini
Layla H. Abood
Anupama Chadha
Nipur Singh
Prashant Kumar
Kuntal Chowdhury
Yogesh Chauhan
Piyush Anand
Michael Albino
Sunil Pathak
Abid Hussain
Sanjeev Kumar
Srikanta Kumar Mohapatra
Gajanand Sharma
Gourav Bathla
Hussein Jabar Khadim

Contents

Wireless Sensor Networks and Computing Technologies

Enhancing QoS of Network Traffic Based on 5G Wireless Networking Using Machine Learning Approaches

Shivani Saini[1(✉)], Sharvan Kumar Garg[1], Pankaj Pratap Singh[2], Arif Ali[2], and Akhilesh Pandey[3]

[1] Subharti Institute of Technology and Engineering, Swami Vivekanand Subharti University, Meerut, India
Shivanisaini792@gmail.com
[2] School of Computer Science and Engineering, Dev Bhoomi Uttarakhand University, Dehradun, India
[3] Uttaranchal School of Computing Science, Uttaranchal University, Dehradun, India

Abstract. 5G wireless networks are based on heterogeneous networks. Heterogeneous networks offer a higher quality of service (QoS) and let you better utilize the resources of the network. Control of traffic on a network is complicated when a multiplicity of heterogeneous networks are present. When different protocols and data transmission rates are used, heterogeneous networks face the problem of managing and managing network traffic appropriately. In this paper our objective is to reduce Network Traffic and improve QoS for 5G wireless Network thus we have discuss some Supervised and Unsupervised Algorithm of Machine Learning Approach. So we have implemented K-mean algorithm in this paper will reduce traffic and improve the efficiency of 5G wireless Network. The K-mean is an iterative grouping technique that moves data objects between cluster sets until one desired set is reached. The dataset for K-mean Algorithm divides the traffic into two classes and then weighted mean is calculated for each cluster until the resultant output is identical weighted mean. If there are two clusters have identical weighted mean then there are no changes in cluster of classes.

Keywords: Heterogeneous network · Traffic classification · Machine learning · Supervised learning · Unsupervised learning

1 Introduction

Now days 5G wireless network run on application that requiring high demand for data rates. Heterogeneous network(HetNets) that can use different power level for transmission to assure the data traffic and heterogeneous utilizes multiple types of access nodes, offers low power consumption, spectrum efficiency, energy efficiency, and quality of service, and offers reduced green house gases. In addition to the conventional" **High power antenna** "HPN and HetNets Introduces **"Low Power Antenna"**. The high power antenna can sever large the geographical area and low power antenna can sever

© The Author(s), under exclusive license to Springer Nature Switzerland AG 2022
R. Mehra et al. (Eds.): ICCISC 2022, CCIS 1672, pp. 3–15, 2022.
https://doi.org/10.1007/978-3-031-22915-2_1

comparatively small the geographical area. Various layers of cells, for example, femto, full scale, miniature, pico, transfers, different client gadgets and applications interface with the heterogeneous organization.

Heterogeneous In wireless telecommunications, network expressions can have a variety of meanings. It could, for example, refer to a pattern of flawless and always-present interoperability among a variety of multi-reporting protocols (HetNet). Alternative uses for the term in homogeneity include describing the spatial division of wireless nodes or users (also known as spatial distribution in homogeneity) [1] (see Fig. 1).

Explains the lack of clarity in technical writing and peer-reviewed publications could result from describing the perception of "heterogeneous networks" without providing that context. Secondary uncertainty may arise as a result of the fact that the "HetNet" pattern can be studied from a "geometric" perspective as well as [2].

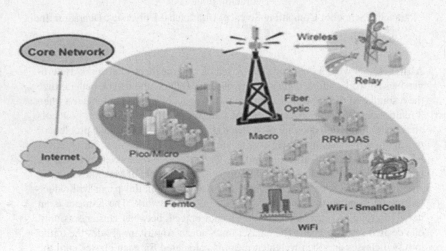

Fig. 1. Heterogeneous network

2   Traffic Classifications

(See Fig. 2) The traffic classification what does mean and why should we are in a word it's all about performance We believe the traffic classification is serious to civilizing your Ethernet. IP Network presentation and the consumer knowledge that is because present simply so much bandwidth presented on your network and present a grouping of traffic like voice and finances transaction application are critical and needs to get through quickly as soon as possible next year may have For other traffic, such as Internet browsing through video streaming this traffic may be less latency sensitive variation and then there all the rest which still needs to get there but can probably wait a bit by classifying traffic before putting on network you make the best use of bandwidth you have available for illustration purpose its compare it an airplane that is only one quarter fall what worse is that you cannot fit all your passengers in the first class on the airplane so bring if another fill up the first again and fly another one quarter full and so on its.

In networking the same with available bandwidth and the network traffic if you're not clarity the traffic before it gets on to the network then all of two gets treated as a priority this doesn't make sense now here what does you take certain traffic and say this is my first class traffic must get through rapidly then this is my business class traffic it can get through rapidly but can wait a little first class need to get through first what remain is my best effort traffic which can wait.

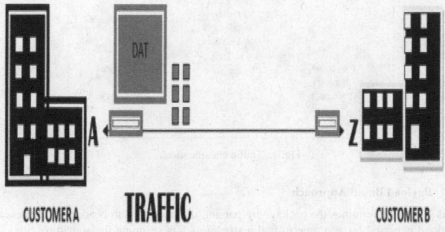

Fig. 2. Traffic classifications

3 Related Works

In (see Fig. 3) its shows Internet Traffic classification is divided into three Approaches are followings.

3.1 Port Based Approach

In a node, many processes will be running and data which are sent or received must reach the right Process. Every Process in a node is uniquely indentified using port number. Suppose in a computer there are five process running and one process is requesting to the data to the another computer replying and that reply must reach the right process which send the request and reaching the right process which has sent the request the right process and reaching the right process which has sent the request is done with help of port address [3]. So, Port number or simply port we called as the communication end point. In real Scenarios we have two categories of port number fixed port number (25.80) and dynamic port number (0–65565).UDP also uses port numbers, even though it is connection less service [4].

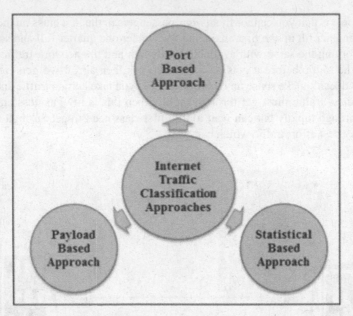

Fig. 3. Traffic classifications

3.2 Payload Based Approach

This method determines the package by parsing the package sub headers. The packet payload is parsed bit at a time to find a stream of bits spanning the signature. Sometimes that flow is decisive. In this case, you can name the set of factors precisely. This machine works continuously to detect P2P traffic and identify system outages [5]. The real downside of this system is that security laws prevent administrators from evaluating the payload. It also requires a lot of flexibility and load preparation for traffic identification devices. It scans the entire payload, requiring significant processing power and capacity limitations [6].

3.3 Statistical Based Classification

The pattern recognition system is dividing into two major modes of operation training and classification. The role of preprocessing module is to segment the required pattern from the given background, remove noise and normalization it's and after other operation, represented the pattern for further processing. On this approach the category of networks is base absolutely on association altitude style and Network protocol performance. This technique relies entirely on discovering and verifying host performance patterns at the transport layer. The advantage of this classification is that it does not require packet payload access [7, 8].

4 Work Flow of Traffic Classification in Networks

This is how network traffic can be classified into different types of site visitor learning based on any parameter [9]. First, it captures the traffic of the community and extracts the characteristics of the chosen information. It after that trains the system using the data sampling system and finally runs the algorithm and computes the outcome (see Fig. 4).

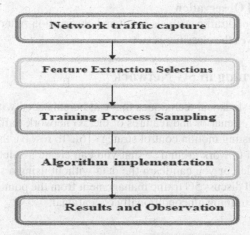

Fig. 4. Traffic classification approaches

STEP: 1 Network Traffic Capture
At this stage of data collection one of the most important and critical step in data collection. This step captures network traffic in real time. There are lots of tools for intercepting network traffic, such as Wire Shark.

STEP: 2 Feature Extraction Selections
The second step in network traffic analysis is the selection of feature extraction. This includes features extracted from the data collected in the first stage of traffic analysis, such as packet length, packet duration, and time between packet arrival protocols, etc. Then use the extract function to train a machine learning class. After training the model and receiving the data, machine learning validates the data and outputs the results accordingly. Some machine learning algorithm classifiers are trained during data testing and training respectively.

STEP: 3 Training Process Sampling
The third step in network traffic analysis is sampling of the learning process. Contains data sets selected for supervised learning. In supervised learning, data are first labeled to classify unfamiliar network applications [10].

STEP: 4 Algorithm Implementation
The fourth step in network traffic analysis is the implementation of machine learning algorithms. Implementation steps involved in applying a machine learning algorithm or classifier to an instance. For example, the use of supervised, unsupervised and semi-supervised learning algorithms. This article implements the algorithm of SVM and naive

Bayes supervised K-Nearest Neighbor algorithm, the unsupervised learning algorithm is K-Means, DBSCAN.

STEP: 5 Results and Observation
The third step of network traffic analysis result and observation.After applying machine learning algorithm gives the classifier result.

5 Machine Learning in 5G Network

ML algorithms using statistical techniques that can be enhanced with experience with the machine. The new scenarios and features of the 5G network traffic described above use many calls for existing motion control strategy [6]. To resolve these problems, you can resolve a solution to work around so that you can create a solution directly to the machine training model, or you can learn the data without using a subsequent rule set [11] (see Fig. 5) is will discuss 5G traffic management from the point of view of the ML algorithm: controlled training, unconditionally educational.

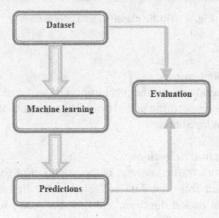

Fig. 5. Machine learning workflow

6 Supervised Learning

Supervised learning is a method which we provide the machine a label dataset or in other word we can say that we provide the machine with a given data set on which it is trained to perform a future task. Supervised learning creates a comprehensive model that maps contribution features to desired outputs. In a number of cases, maps are implemented as a set of limited models, such because case-based inference or Nearest-Neighbor algorithms.

Supervised learning applied to network management has been reported to shape network routing path selection, traffic volume prediction, etc. [12]. To solve the 5G network traffic problem with supervised learning, you should consider the following steps:

Step 1: Decide on the type of string example.
Step 2: Assemble the training set.
Step 3: Determine the input representation of the recognizable function.
Step 4: It determines the structure of the well-read function and the algorithm for learning it.

6.1 Supervised Learning Algorithm

These are the supervised machine learning algorithms following:

a) Naïve Bayes
b) Support Vector Machine
c) K-Nearest Neighbor

6.2 Naïve Bayes

Naive Bayes Most of the generic Bayesian network models used for machine learning. Bayes' theorem is used to manage network traffic and accurately classifies network traffic using flow features provided as training data for the model. Naive Bayesian learning has no problems with noisy data and can make more accurate predictions (See Fig. 6).

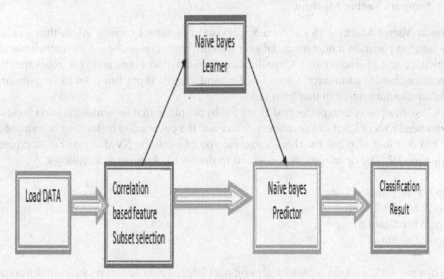

Fig. 6. Naïve Bayes work flow

Step 1: Read the dataset (Collection of IP address)
Step 2: Correlation Based Feature Selection (Relationship-based element subset selection is used in studies to find subsets of highlights with high-level explicit relationships and low-level relationships.)

Step 3: Naïve Bayes Learner (learn the naïve bayes model).
Step 4: Naïve Bayes Predictor (Use Naïve Bayes model to predict classes)
Step 5: Classification Result.

6.3 K-Nearest Neighbor

The nearest neighbor rule is an extension of the nearest neighbor rule. Most classes of these K nearest neighbors are class labels assigned to the new sample. The value chosen for k is significant. If the value of k is correct, the classification accuracy is better than using the nearest-neighbor algorithm.

Networks can assign cluster values and use K-Nearest Neighbors to classify traffic. In the K-nearest neighbor method, K can be any integer greater than one. Calculate the nearest neighbor group for each new data point to classify.

There are flowing step in K – nearest neighbor.

Steps 1: Get data.
Steps 2: Define K Neighbors.
Steps 3: Calculated the Neighbors Distance.
Steps 4: Assign new instance to Majority of Neighbors.

6.4 Support Vector Machine

Support Vector Machine (SVM) is a Supervised Machine Learning Algorithm generally used to partition a numerical data set into different classes based on mathematical properties and characteristics. Classification aims to find constraints (or equivalently minimize classification errors) between different classes using limits on the maximum distance from a sample to that limit [13].

Classification is then performed along the hyper plane that separates the two classes. If you need a model that can accurately determine if a cat is a dog by looking at a strange cat and dog that also has cat characteristics, you can use the SVM algorithm to create such a model. The development concerned in the SVM classifier is as follows:

Step1: Past Labeled Data.
Step 2: Model Training.
Step 3: Predication.
Step 4: Output.

In a network, first the network trains on past labeled data so that it can learn different characteristics of the data, It then tests the new data and after that learns how the algorithm predicts and classifies new received classes. You need to prepare the classifier first and in that case cross-validate it through the data validation. To get correct predictions with the SVM classifier, you want to utilize the SVM kernel purpose and tune the parameters.

7 Unsupervised Learning Algorithm

This is learning to train an output device to respond to a group of patterns as input. Unsupervised learning is used in self-organizing neural networks. You don't need a teacher for this training. In this learning method, Related types of input vectors are grouped mutually not including by means of tanning data to point out what a representative component of every one grouping capacity look like, or which group a component belongs to. During training, the neural network receives input models and classifies them. When a new input model is applied, the neural network provides an output response indicating which class the input model belongs to. If no class exists for the input model, a new class is created.

The study of network traffic management in 5G networks allows the use of traffic patterns and probabilistic modeling in traffic conditions. Network planning and configuration, network traffic, better network planning and configuration forecasting. Failure of hands-free algorithms used in networks – K-Mean, DBSCAN.

7.1 K-Mean

The K-mean is an iterative grouping technique that moves data objects between cluster sets until one desired set is reached.A tall degree of similitude is accomplished between components of a cluster, whereas a tall degree of disparity between components of diverse clusters is accomplished at the same time.

a) Algorithm
A K-mean partitioning algorithm that expresses the centered of each cluster as the average of the features in the cluster.
   K = Number of clusters.
   $D = \{t_1, t_2, \dots t_n\}$:An data set contain n objects.
   Output: A set of K Clusters.

b) Method

1) Arbitrary in D, select K features as initial cluster centroids.
2) Replicate
3) (re) allocate all object ti in the cluster where the object is nearly all related, It is based on the average value of the objects in the cluster and Update the cluster mean. Analyze the average of the features for each cluster.
4) Repeated pending there is rejection adjusts.

c) Proposed Model for Reduced Network Traffic
Ts = Traffic state.
K = Number of clusters.
M = weighted Mean.

i.   Suppose that we have given the following traffic states to cluster. (2Ts1, 4Ts2, 10Ts3, 12Ts4, 3Ts5, 20Ts6, 30TS7,11Ts8, 25Ts9,) and K = 2.

ii.   We initially assign th means to the first two values M1 = 2 and M2 = 4.
iii.   Using Euclidean distance initially K1 = {2Ts1, 3Ts5} and K2 = {4Ts2, 10Ts3, 12Ts4, 20Ts6, 30TS7, 11Ts8, 25Ts9}
iv.   The Value 3 is equidistant from both means, so K1 is arbitrarily chosen.
v.   Now, means are recalculated to get M1 = 2.5, and M2 = 16.
vi.   Objects are assigned again to the crew clusters having K1 = {2Ts1, 3Ts5, 4Ts2} and K2 = {10Ts3, 12Ts4, 20Ts6, 30TS7, 11Ts8, 25Ts9,} Continuing this we obtain the following.
vii.   The clusters in the last two steps are identical.
viii. This will yield identical means and thus the means same and no changes in clusters.

This will provide identical and therefore identical means and no variation in clusters (Figs. 7, 8, 9 and 10) (Table 1).

Table. 1. Variation in clusters

M_1	M_2	K_1	K_2
3	18	$\{2Ts_1, 3Ts_5, 4Ts_2, 10Ts_3\}$	$\{20Ts_6, 30T_{S7}, 11Ts_8, 25Ts_9\}$
4.75	19.6	$\{2Ts_1, 3Ts_5, 4Ts_2, 10Ts_3, 11Ts_8, 12Ts_4\}$	$\{20Ts_6, 30T_{S7}, 25Ts_9\}$
7	25	$\{2Ts_1, 3Ts_5, 4Ts_2, 10Ts_3, 11Ts_8, 12Ts_4\}$	$\{20Ts_6, 30T_{S7}, 25Ts_9\}$

7.2 DBSCAN

Noise-based spatial density clustering is a density-based clustering algorithm that uses dense functional areas. Parameters used in the DBSCAN algorithm.

Esp, score, minimum DBSCAN clusters reach the density directly and are formed at the midpoint where the density can be reached. Collect data from online tools, select features based on the package, and adapt your model to testing and training. Finally, forecasts and reviews.

Let X = {x1, x2, x3, …, xn} be the set of data points. DBSCAN requires two.
Parameters: (eps) and the smallest number of points needed to.
Form a cluster (Minpts).

1) The algorithm proceeds by randomly selecting a point from the data set (waiting for all points to have been accessed. Access).
2) If there are at smallest amount 'minPoint' points inside the radius 'ε' Up to this point, all these points are considered part of the same cluster
3) Then the clusters are extended by how to recursively iterate the neighborhood calculating for both neighbor point.

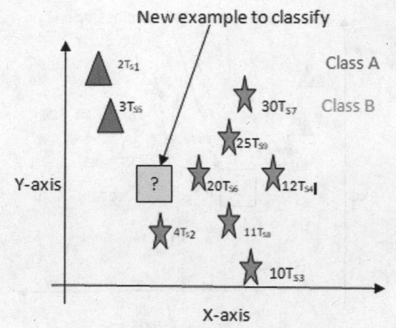

Fig. 7. Initial data (K = 2)

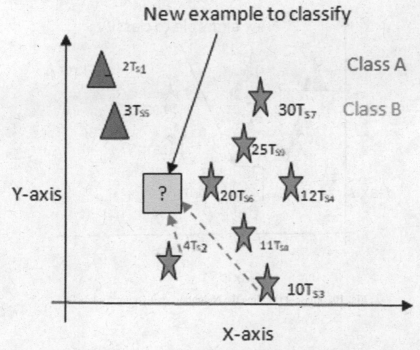

Fig. 8. Phase – 2 (Finding the Neighbors and voting for label)

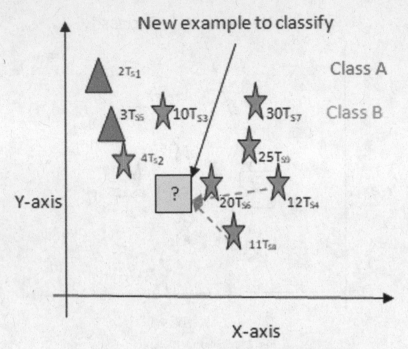

Fig. 9. Phase -3 (Finding the Neighbors and voting for label)

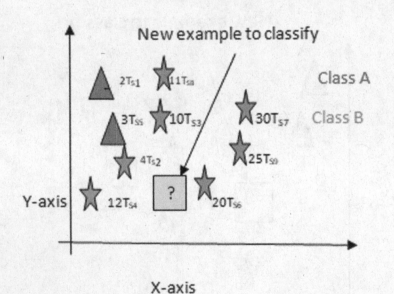

Fig. 10. Phase-4 (Finding the Neighbors and voting for label)

8 Conclusions

Heterogeneous networks are the foundation of 5G networks when traffic on the network plays a major role in disrupting network performance. This article described ML for 5G traffic control, including supervised and unsupervised learning. Supervised learning algorithm. When we use Naive Bayes algorithm its provide less accuracy because If there is a variable in the test dataset that is not in the tan dataset, the naive Bayes model assigns it a probability of zero and makes no predictions about it and Support vector Machine is not appropriate for huge amount of dataset for the reason that of its high training time and SVM performance was not good in case of overlapping classes. In unsupervised learning algorithm we using the k-mean algorithm are used reduce the network traffic using the method Clustering that gives the more accuracy.

References

1. Soldani, D., Manzalini, A.: Horizon 2020 and beyond: on the5G operating system for a true digital society. IEEE Veh. Technol. Mag. **10**(1), 32–42 (2015)
2. Liu, Y., Zhang, Y., Yu, R., Xie, S.: Integrated energy and spectrum harvesting for 5G wireless communications. IEEE Network **29**(3), 75–81 (2015)
3. Shafi, M., et al.: 5G: A tutorial overview of standards, trials, challenges, deployment, and practice. IEEE JSAC **35**(6), 1201–1221 (2017)
4. Dhote, Y., Agrawal, S., Deen, A.J.: A survey on feature selection techniques for internet traffic classification. In: 2015 International Conference on Computational Intelligence and Communication Networks (CICN). IEEE (2015)
5. Dzulkifly, S., Giupponi, L., Sai, F., Dohler, M.: Decentralized Q learning for uplink power control. In: IEEE International Workshop on Computer Aided Modelling and Design of Communication Links and Networks, pp. 54–58. IEEE (2015)
6. Li, R., et al.: Intelligent 5G: when cellular networks meet artificial intelligence. IEEE Wirel. Commun. **24**, 175–183 (2017)
7. Alnwaimi, G., Vahid, S., Moessner, K.: Dynamic heterogeneous learning games for opportunistic access in LTE-based macro/femtocell deployments. IEEE Trans. Wirel. Commun. **14**(4), 2294–2308 (2015)
8. Challita, U., Dong, L., Saad, W.: Deep learning for proactive resource allocation in LTE-U networks. In: European Wireless 2017- 23rd European Wireless Conference (2017)
9. Shafiq, M., et al.: Network traffic classification techniques and comparative analysis using machine learning algorithms. In: 2016 2nd IEEE International Conference on Computer and Communications (ICCC). IEEE (2016)
10. Mole, P.V.: Towards 5G Enabled Traffic Management Systems: A Literature Review
11. Chih-Lin, I., Han, S., Xu, Z., Wang, S., Sun, Q., Chen, Y.: New paradigm of 5G wireless internet. IEEE J. Sel. Areas in Commun. **34**(3), 474–482 (2016)
12. Fu, Y., et al.: Artificial intelligence to manage network traffic of 5G wireless networks. IEEE Network **32**(6), 58–64 (2018)
13. Chiti, F., Fantacci, R., Giuli, D., Paganelli, F., Rigazzi, G.: Communications protocol design for 5G vehicular networks. In: Xiang, W., Zheng, K., Shen, X.((eds.) 5G mobile communications, pp. 625–649. Springer, Cham (2017). https://doi.org/10.1007/978-3-319-34208-5_23

Soil Classification and Crop Prediction Using Machine Learning

Yuvraj Jangir[✉], Tushar Goyal, Sumit Kandari, and Arshad Husain

Department of Computer Science, DIT University, Dehradun, Uttarakhand, India
Yuv.rraj786@gmail.com

Abstract. Soil classification is the process in which soil is segregated according to its physical and chemical properties. This process can be achieved manually or using a machine learning algorithm. The use of machine learning algorithms has been on the rise in recent years due to their accuracy. They can classify soils with more precision than humans can manually, by considering many factors such as pH, organic matter content, and particle size distribution. We here proposed a model to classify soil and to predict the most suitable crops using various algorithms of machine learning like Convolutional Neural networks (CNN), Decision Trees, Naive Bayes. Soil and crop datasets are used, they comprise of different geographical and physical. Parameters. The module is tested on manually created datasets and results are obtained.

Keywords: Soil types · Machine learning · Convolutional neural network (CNN) · Decision tree classifier

1 Introduction

1.1 Objective of Study

To alleviate the agricultural crisis in its current state, it is necessary to put in place better recommendation systems to alleviate the crisis by helping farmers make informed decisions before planting begins. The main objective of this experiment was to classify and predict the suitability of different types of soils on various crops based on predictor variables like temperature, rainfall, and location. Prediction obtained using decision trees algorithm. It is important to note that this algorithm works only when a set number of input values are set up in the form of training samples, which gives a result prediction for each sample in accordance with that input setting, which can then be compared against ground truth at other input settings (some samples may not have the rule applicable). As such, each predictor variable was considered as a feature to define the suitability of a given map. A decision tree was then constructed to mimic this process and so predict the result for an input location.

© The Author(s), under exclusive license to Springer Nature Switzerland AG 2022
R. Mehra et al. (Eds.): ICCISC 2022, CCIS 1672, pp. 16–21, 2022.
https://doi.org/10.1007/978-3-031-22915-2_2

1.2   Related Works

In order to predicts soil type and based on the prediction, suggests suitable a model is proposed which includes several machine learning algorithms are used for soil classification. Experimental results show that the proposed SVM (support vector machines) based method performs better than many existing methods [1]. Soil dataset ánd crop dataset were used to classify the soil. Soil dataset contains class labelled chemical feature of soil. The crop suggestion dataset contains class labelled crop suggestion attributes [2]. The soil image has been analyzed using various image preprocessing. Soil color is identified using statistical properties such as mean of Red, Blue, Green (RGB) values of image pixels. A classification of soil based on feature extraction of soil color, soil pH values and texture by using Support Vector Machine classifier. Here, the one-against-all SVM method is used for classification. Recommended which crops were suitable for tested soil image based on feature extraction by using image processing [3]. Digital image processing and Image analysis technology has been used in which suggestions of crops to be grown in that soil type. The image of the soil/land is clicked using phone camera and submit it. An Image is a two - dimensional signal. Image processing is a method to perform some operations on an image, to get an enhanced image or to extract some useful information [4]. A model has been proposed for predicting the soil type and suggesting a suitable crop that can be cultivated in that soil. The model predicts soil fertility and 8 other properties of agricultural land [5]. A comprehensive system is described for soil classification in which different images of soil samples are captured. The features of each type of soil are collected and are stored in a separate database. This database is later used in the final stage for soil classification [6]. In order to efficiently classify the soil instances and maps the soil type to the crop data to get better prediction with higher accuracies. Soil prediction involves types of crop classifications and geographical attributes. It also aims at creating a system that processes the real-time soil data to predict the crops with higher accuracy [7].

2   Proposed Framework

In present work, we propose a novel methodology for soil classification using Convolutional Neural Network (CNN). (Fig. 1.) The generated classifiers were validated with the accuracy of more than 90%. Secondly, we discussed about crop prediction using decision tree-based classifier.

In this paper, we described a proposed architecture for soil classification using image samples. Soil classification is done by analyzing different types of soil image samples. Enough training samples are needed to classify soil samples. Training samples should be selected carefully. After selecting the training dataset, all the images are then passed through Image Processing which includes resizing and augmentation process. After applying Image Processing on all images, the resultant images are passed through Convolutional Neural Network (CNN) for classification.

Convolutional Neural Network (CNN) Is a powerful algorithm for image processing. These algorithms are currently the best algorithms we have for the automated processing of images. CNN is a directed acyclic graph with four main layers, which are: input layer,

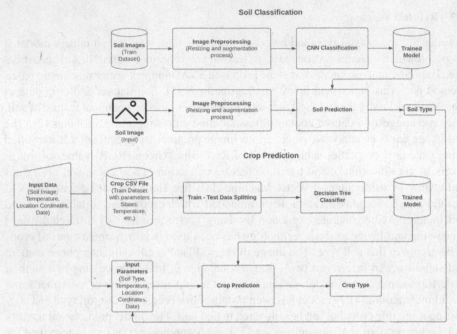

Fig. 1. Architecture of the system

filter layer (convolutional layer), pooling layer and output layer to provide better accuracy of classification. CNN is used to classify the soil samples by extracting various features from the image. (Fig. 2.) The dataset used in the paper contains nearly 200 cropped images from different soil types. It is a type of machine learning algorithm that allows for classification and prediction tasks. It is used to classify inputs into several categories and predict an output based on given inputs. Images contain data of RGB combination. The computer does not see an image, all it sees is an array of numbers. Color images are stored in 3-dimensional arrays. The first two dimensions correspond to the height and width of the image (the number of pixels). The last dimension corresponds to the red, green, and blue colors present in each pixel.

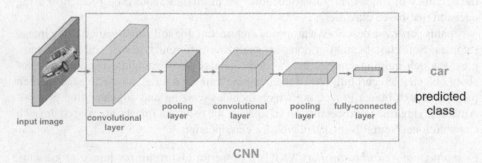

Fig. 2. Working of CNN

The output of CNN is compared with a threshold value and if it is greater than the threshold value then it will be classified into class1 otherwise it will be classified into class2. The classification process is done using Python 3.10.4 and Keras 2.8.0 lucid framework. The evaluated accuracy of this method is greater than 90%, which means the method is reliable, accurate and fast. Then, the trained model is stored in h5 format, which is then used to predict the soil, using the image provided in the input.

In the crop prediction model, we first created a dataset with the following parameters: states, rainfall, ground water, temperature, soil type, season, and crop, and stored it in a csv file. After creating the dataset, we split the data for the training data set and the testing data set separately. After that, we used the decision tree classifier to train the crop prediction model. The performance of the model was measured by the accuracy value.

Decision Tree Is a supervised prediction method which is widely used because they can easily obtain input data and are suitable for classifying the data into a wide range of categories. Decision trees can be used as a type of classifier or regression model that uses binary trees to predict outcomes. The key advantage of decision trees is that they can be easily implemented and interpreted. Decision tree models have been shown to be effective in many real-world applications. Decision tree classifiers are used in many fields, such as pattern recognition, data mining, machine learning and bioinformatics. Decision trees can be used to predict categorical outcomes, and they frequently have an option to do regression functions.

In this study, we presented a real-world dataset that has the names of various crops. We also had the opportunity to determine two meteorological inputs: rainfall and ground water level. These two inputs were necessary to help us build a crop prediction model using decision trees. After training the model, we stored the model in a.sav format, which is then used to predict the crop, using the parameters provided in the input and the soil type predicted using soil classification model.

3 Result and Discussion

3.1 Dataset Collection

Multiple datasets are used to train and obtain relevant results. All the datasets used are custom datasets; built and structured according to the requirements of the algorithm and the proposed test cases. Below is the list and types of the datasets used-

1. *Soils.zip (Soil Image Dataset)* - Contains about 150–200 images of different types of soil which are used for agriculture and found in the Indian subcontinent.
2. *Cat_crops.csv* - The CSV file mentioned contains data on various parameters that were considered when training the machine learning model for the crop recommendation system.

```
19/19 [==============================] - 5s 281ms/step - loss: 0.4118 - acc: 0.8564
Epoch 19/30
19/19 [==============================] - 5s 269ms/step - loss: 0.5900 - acc: 0.7790
Epoch 20/30
19/19 [==============================] - 5s 259ms/step - loss: 0.4046 - acc: 0.8232
Epoch 21/30
19/19 [==============================] - 5s 276ms/step - loss: 0.4455 - acc: 0.8453
Epoch 22/30
19/19 [==============================] - 5s 257ms/step - loss: 0.2921 - acc: 0.8508
Epoch 23/30
19/19 [==============================] - 5s 265ms/step - loss: 0.3423 - acc: 0.8508
Epoch 24/30
19/19 [==============================] - 5s 260ms/step - loss: 0.4867 - acc: 0.8508
Epoch 25/30
19/19 [==============================] - 6s 294ms/step - loss: 0.2686 - acc: 0.9061
Epoch 26/30
19/19 [==============================] - 5s 260ms/step - loss: 0.1788 - acc: 0.9227
Epoch 27/30
19/19 [==============================] - 5s 263ms/step - loss: 0.4485 - acc: 0.8343
Epoch 28/30
19/19 [==============================] - 5s 268ms/step - loss: 0.1840 - acc: 0.9392
Epoch 29/30
19/19 [==============================] - 5s 267ms/step - loss: 0.3575 - acc: 0.8674
Epoch 30/30
19/19 [==============================] - 5s 262ms/step - loss: 0.2099 - acc: 0.9227
```

Fig. 3. Result obtained

3.2 Results

The below Fig. 3. Represents the accuracy of the soil classification model which was built using CNN (Convolutional Neural Networks).

After several changes and observations, it has been noticed that after improving the dataset, the accuracy of the model is also improved.

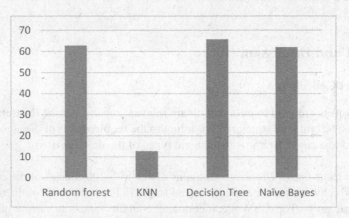

Fig. 4. Accuracy of different algorithm

In crop prediction model, we provided a csv file which consists of the following parameters: States, Rainfall, Ground Water, Temperature, Soil Type, Season and Crop. We compared the results with the previous prediction methods. (see Fig. 4.) We used 4 different classifiers to train the crop prediction model, out of which the decision tree classifier gave us the best accuracy among them. The accuracies of all the different classifiers used were:

4   Conclusions and Future Scope

This proposed system is based on an image processing technique where digital images of the soil samples were processed using convolutional neural network (CNN). In this study, Decision Tree was used to determine the crop suitability of the soil sample. The results showed that CNN recommended which crops were suitable for tested image of the soil samples. So, the proposed method will help farmers to increase the productivity of yield by identifying suitable crops for the soil samples.

In future perspective, a point location-based rainfall prediction and ground water detection module can be integrated with the other parameters. This would increase the overall prediction of suitable crops. Also, the dataset for all these three experiments consisted of nearly 200 cropped images from different soil types, a larger dataset is needed. This will increase the accuracy of prediction and classification of soil as well as crop.

References

1. Rahman, S.A.Z., Mitra, K.C., Islam, S.M.M.: Soil classification using machine learning methods and crop suggestion based on soil series. In: International Conference of Science and Technology Computer (2018)
2. Reddy, K.M.A., Chithra, S., Hemashree, H.M., Kurian, T.: Soil classification and crop Yadav, suggestion. Int. J. Res. Appl. Sci. Eng. Technol. (2020)
3. Yadav, P., Ahire, P.: Soil health analysis for crop suggestions using machine learning. AEGAEUM J. (2020)
4. Aishwarya, M., Revathy, R., Periasamy, J.K., Srujana, T.: Soil classification and crop suggestion using machine learning techniques. J. Gujrat Res. Soc. (2019)
5. Saranya, N., Mythili, A.: Classification of soil and crop suggestion using machine learning techniques. Int. J. Eng. Res. Technol. **9**, 671–673 (2020)
6. Chandan, R.T.: An intelligent model for indian soil classification using various machine learning techniques. Int. J. Comput. Eng. Res. (IJCER) **33**, 3005 (2018)
7. Shravani, V., Uday Kiran, S., Yashaswini, J.S., Priyanka, D.: Soil classification and crop suggestion using machine learning. Int. Res. J. Eng. Technol. (IRJET) (2020)

Analysis of the Performance of Data Mining Classification Algorithm for Diabetes Prediction

Vijaylakshmi Sajwan[1] , Monisha Awasthi[1]([✉]) , Prakhar Awasthi[2] , Ankur Goel[3] , Manisha Khanduja[1] , and Anuj Kumar[4]

[1] Uttaranchal School of Computing Sciences, Uttaranchal University, Dehradun, India
uumonishaawasthi@gmail.com
[2] Department of Computer Science and Engineering, RIT, Bangaluru, Karnataka, India
[3] Department of Business Administration, MIET Group, MIT, Meerut, U.P, India
[4] Uttaranchal Institute of Technology, Uttaranchal Unversity, Dehradun, India

Abstract. The purpose of this paper is to identify solutions for the diagnosis of diabetes disease by analyzing the patterns found in the data using classification algorithms such as Decision Tree, SVM, KNN, Naive Bayes, Random Forest, Neural Network, and Logistic Regression. According to a WHO report, almost 42.2 crores population of the world has diabetes, who are primarily the residents of low and middle income countries, and diabetes is resulting in around 0.15 crores of deaths each year globally [1]. To evaluate and discuss the performance of above-mentioned algorithms, Orange as a data mining tool has been applied. Furthermore, the data set used in this research is the "Pima Indian Diabetic Dataset," which is obtained from the University of California, Irvine (UCI) Repository of Machine Learning datasets. As this study utilized several classifiers to simulate actual diabetes diagnosis for local and systemic therapy, the results indicated that Logistic Regression outperforms all other classifiers. The experimental data also demonstrated the significance of the suggested model in the study. The disease has been ranked as the fifth-deadliest in the United States, and there is currently no cure in sight. With the advancement of information technology and its continued penetration into the medical and healthcare sectors, diabetes cases and symptoms have become well documented and discussed. The research is original and adds value to the current studies in the same domain as researchers develop a more rapid and efficient method of diagnosing the disease, allowing for more timely treatment of patients.

Keywords: Accuracy · Diabetes · KNN · Logistic regression · Naive bayes · Neural network · Random forest · Support vector machine

1 Introduction

Databases are densely packed with hidden data and are designed to aid in intellectual decision making. Different types of data analysis, such as classification and prediction, are used to make predictions about future data and to describe the data classes. The classification is a process that predicts the labels for categorical classes. The labels for

© The Author(s), under exclusive license to Springer Nature Switzerland AG 2022
R. Mehra et al. (Eds.): ICCISC 2022, CCIS 1672, pp. 22–36, 2022.
https://doi.org/10.1007/978-3-031-22915-2_3

this class may be discrete or nominal in nature. Classification techniques classify data using a training set and class labels [2]. With the rising prevalence of implementations of various classification and prediction algorithms, there is a need for a central hub that could evaluate the performance of all classification algorithms as well as provide information on which classifier is the best [3].

The objective here is to examine various algorithms of machine learning for classification using the diabetes data set. ORANGE is also used for this purpose. The purpose of this paper is to compare ORANGE classifiers on a diabetes dataset. Such techniques are compared using the results of their ORANGE calculations. We have used the Diabetes dataset because it is a chronic and one of the dramatically increasing metabolic diseases in the world. Diabetes mellitus, more generally referred to as diabetes, is a collection of illnesses (metabolic) characterized by persistently increased levels of sugar in a blood (beyond a certain limit) and caused by lowering the secretion of insulin or biological effects, or both. It is a disorder in which the person's body is not able to metabolize food in an adequate manner. Diabetes can wreak havoc on a variety of tissues, most notably the eyes, kidneys, heart, blood vessels, and nerves, resulting in chronic damage and dysfunction. Diabetes is primarily classified into two segments (types): T1D – Type 1 Diabetes and T2D - Type 2 Diabetes. Type 1 diabetes typically develops in young aged people (below 30 years of age), and the general symptoms include thirst and urination again, as well as elevated levels of sugar in the blood. Only must be treated with insulin as impossible with other oral drugs. Type 2 diabetes is more prevalent in the younger than younger aged and senior population, and is frequently related with obesity, hypertension, dyslipidemia, arteriosclerosis, and other disorders [4]. Numerous data mining classification methods have been developed with the goal of classifying, forecasting, and diagnosing diabetes. However, no meaningful comparison evaluation of the performance of such algorithms has been conducted. There has been no research conducted to determine which of the existing classifier model scans provides the best prediction for diabetes. The decision tree, Naive Bayes, Random Forest, KNN (K-Nearest neighbours) and Support vector machines (SVM) classification methods were utilized in this work to develop classifier models [5].

2 Related Work

According to Aljumah [6], diabetes is a chronic condition that arises when the body insulin is ineffectively used or when the pancreas produces insufficient insulin. A prominent hormone, Insulin regulates the levels of blood sugar. Unregulated diabetes results in a rise of blood sugar, which leads to serious vandalism to various body parts and systems, like the blood vessels and nerves, over time. According to Health informatics, it is the study of how to collect, retrieve, communicate, store, and utilize health-related data, knowledge, and information to the best of one's ability. Barakat et al. [7] defined how healthcare providers should handle patient information and how citizens should participate in their own health care. It is now widely recognized as a necessary and widespread component of long-term health-care delivery. Machine Learning (ML) is the fastest-growing area in computer science today. When using machine learning in diabetes related data for prediction, it's important to remember that this data isn't being collected to address specific research questions; instead, learning algorithms are being utilized to analyze biomedical data automatically. Song et al. [8] analyzed multiple categorization algorithms utilizing characteristics such as thickness of skin, pedigree of diabetes, glucose level, Body Mass Index, patient age, insulin and blood pressure. Pradeep and Dr. Naveen compared the machine learning algorithms' performances in [9] and measured the accuracy of each algorithm. There were accuracy variations in terms of techniques utilized, pre-processing and after processing of data. It was noticed that 'Pre-processing of data' had better accuracy and overall performance for prediction of diabetes. In this study, before preprocessing for prediction of diabetes, the Decision tree algorithm provided better accuracy as compared to other techniques like Random forest and Support vector machine. According to Loannis et al. [10], Machine learning techniques, such as the diabetic disorders dataset, have become a significant tool for predicting diabetes using diverse medical data sets (DD). In this work, SVM, Logistic Regression, and Nave Bayes were used. They used 10-fold cross validation for the diabetes dataset (DD). The SVM (Support Vector Machine) strategy outperformed the others in terms of precision and processing, according to the study. For diabetes prediction, Nilashi et al. [11] suggested a CART (classification and Regression Tree) model. Expectation Maximization (EM) and PCA (Principal Component Analysis) were applied to pre-process the data and remove noise before applying the rule. The goal of this study is to design a diabetes decision assistance system. The effect of CART with removal of noise provided efficiency and enhanced prediction, allowing human life to be saved from premature demise. A categorization model was suggested by Kamadi et al. in [12]. One of the most typical problems in categorization, they claim, is reduction of data. PCA (principal component Analysis) was employed in this work for pre-processing of data, as well as for reduction of data to enhance accuracy. The study employed a modified DT (Decision tree) and a fuzzy rule to make predictions. They discovered that reducing the dataset improves the results. Sajida et al. [13] employed the Canadian primary care sentinel surveillance Network(CPCSSN) dataset and three machine learning models to detect diabetes at a primary stage in order to save human lives. To predict diabetes, decision tree (J48), Adaboost, and Bagging were used in this study. Rathore et al. [14] Diabetic disorder can be detected and predicted. The performance measurements were examined using R Studio and the Pima Indians diabetes dataset. SVM and Decision Tree are two machine learning techniques employed. The SVM has an accuracy of 82%.

In [15], S M Hasan Mahmud et al. forecast diabetes. To discover the performance measurements of the classification algorithms, 10-fold cross validation procedures were used. The study found that Naive Bayes outperformed the other classifiers, with an F1 score of 0.74. On the PIMA dataset, Ahuja et al. [16] conducted a comparison examination of various machine learning techniques, including NB, DT, and MLP, for diabetic categorization and found MLP to be superior to other classifiers. Fine-tuning and efficient feature engineering, according to the authors, can improve MLP's performance. Garca-Ordás, M.T. et al. [17] employ min-max normalization and a variant auto encoder sparse auto encoder to solve data standardization, feature augmentation and imbalance. MLP was then used for classification, with an accuracy of 92.31%. Without preprocessing, Bukhari, M.M. et al. [18] state that their ABP-SCGNN (Artificial Back Propagation Scaled Conjugate Gradient Neural Network) obtained 93% accuracy. [19]

is another example of good performance utilizing NN-based models. They looked at median value imputation (MVI), KNN and an iterative imputer for imputation of the missing value. Then, to attain an F1-score of 98%, MLP was employed for classification. Khanam and Foo [20] employed MVI and Pearson Correlation for selection of features and missing value imputation. To further standardize the data and eliminate outliers, interquartile ranges were used. The classification model based on DNN achieved an accuracy of 88.6% using several hidden layers. Overall, missing value imputation and feature selection regarding data pretreatment techniques were seen to be highly appropriate for prediction of diabetes classification performance. The majority of data preparation approaches, on the other hand, have been found to perform well when data is normally distributed. Nonlinear approaches will be better adapted to the problem if the data does not conform to normalcy assumptions, and they are likely to add significantly to a classifier's performance. As a result, this study will look at nonlinear preprocessing approaches and classifiers for data preprocessing.

3   Methodology

This section describes the classification model's approach as well as its efficacy in DM classification. Figure 1 summarises the process.

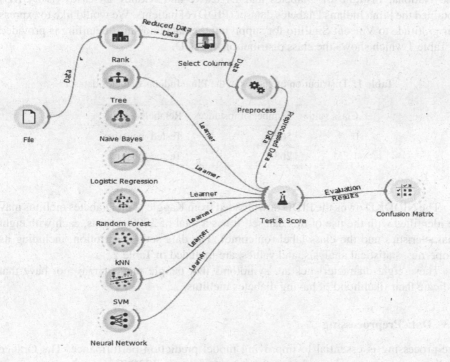

Fig. 1. Methodology of proposed work

For all of the algorithms (Naive Bayes, KNN,ANN, Logistic Regression,Decision Tree, Random Forest, SVM), the 'Confusion Matrix (CM)' encapsulates the various steps from raw data to grading, data reduction, pre-processing, scoring, and testing.These steps are described in greater detail in the following subsections as:

A- It describes the data mining toolkit.
B- It describes the database and its attributes.
C- It provides insights into the pre-processing steps.
D- It discusses the process of classification using the algorithms of seven classifications.

3.1 Data Mining Toolkit

To imitate excellent classification techniques, the Orange Data Mining suite of tools [21] is utilized. Orange was developed as an Open Source Machine Learning (OSML) framework having in-built visualization of data and analytic capabilities at the University of Ljubljana's Bioinformatics Lab. Orange provides a data preprocessing, classification, regression, clustering, visualization and assessment environment with association rules.

3.2 Collection of Database

The National Institute of Diabetes and Digestive and Kidney Diseases (NIDDKD) obtained the Pima Indians Diabetes dataset (PIDD) of patients. We would like to express our gratitude to Vincent Sigillito for supplying the data and short detailing is provided in Table 1 which shows the class distribution in PIDD.

Table 1. Distribution of classes in the Pima Indians diabetes dataset

Class value	Number of instances	Relabeled value
0	500	Tested_negative
1	268	Tested_positive

The NIDDKD owns the PIDD downloaded from Kaggle [22]. Diabetes mellitus may be identified with the use of this dataset. It has a total of 2000 records, each with eight characteristics and the class label (outcome). The data set's description, including its properties, statistical analysis, and values, are included in Table 2.

These eight characteristics are symptoms that people may or may not have that indicate their likelihood of having diabetes mellitus.

3.3 Data Preprocessing

Pre-processing is essential to improving model prediction performance. The Orange toolbox supports a variety of pre-processing techniques [23]. Three different types of pre-processing approaches are used in this article to increase the dataset's quality and eventually the classification models performance.

Table 2. Data set description, properties, statistical analysis and values of data

S No	Attribute name	Attribute description	Data type of attribute	Range of attribute
1	Preg	Pregnancy frequency	N	0 to 17
2	Plas	Concentration of Plasma Glucose	N	0 to199
3	Pres	BP (Blood Pressure) (mm, hg)	N	0 to 122
4	Skin	Thickness of skin fold	N	0 to 99
5	Insulin	2 h serum insulin (mm U/ml	N	0 to 846
6	Mass	BMI – Body Mass Index	N	0 to 67.1
7	Pedi	Function of Diabetes pedigree	N	0.078 to 2.42
8	Age	Age of Person (in yrs.)	N	21 to 81
9	Outcome	Class variable	....	Tested positive, tested negative

N* - Numeric

- Removal of values which are missing

Due to the fact that the utilized dataset had some missing values, Orange toolkit presents three methods for imputing values which are missing: eliminate such records, change them with values which are random, or lastly, change such values with the mean of other accessible values [24]. As a result, this strategy is selected to be utilized to eliminate missing values from the applied dataset.

- Selection of Relevant feature

It is critical to choose the most relevant elements. This stage assigns a score to each characteristic based on its association with the designated diabetes class. From the dataset, eight characteristics were retrieved. ANOVA is a statistical technique. [25] Once ANOVA was calculated, it was obtained that thickness of skin and BP are the least important characteristics and would play a little role in the process of classification; hence, they were deleted from the features vector, resulting in six rather than eight features. Figure 2. The table below summarizes the results of the ANOVA test on the characteristics.

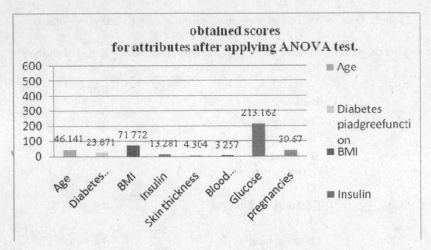

Fig. 2. Result of ANOVA test on the characteristics

- Normalize the Data

Normalization of data can simplify operations and increase computation performance. As a result, the data were normalized to a general scale in a range of zero and one [26]. Scaling by standard deviation (SD) is one of the methods provided in the Orange toolbox.

3.4 Data Classification

During this step, the diabetes dataset was classified using six different algorithms. The investigated classifiers were Naive Bayes, KNN, ANN, SVM, Random Forest, Decision Tree, Logistic Regression and Adaboost. The data set of features in the data base is separated into two parts as training was 70% and testing was 30% to guarantee that the classification process is exactly fit.

- Naive Bayes

Naive Bayes is a statistical learning technique that uses a condensed version of the Bayes rule to determine the posterior distribution of a category given the input attribute values of an example case. Prior probabilities for groups and attribute values that are conditional on categories are calculated using training data frequency counts. Naive Bayes is a straightforward and fast technique for learning that frequently beats more advanced methods. Bayesian classification is both a supervised learning technique and a statistical classification technique. It is capable of resolving diagnostic and predictive issues [27].

- KNN

The KNN algorithm [28] is a simple classification approach. The detection of the nearest K neighbours during the training phase. The distance between objects and the value of K, the number of closest neighbours, are calculated using a similarity measure.

- ANN

ANN is a supervised learning method [29] that uses a network of layers to represent input data, one or more non-linear layers called hidden layers, and finally an output layer that represents the classification category.

- Random Forest

This classifier creates a collection of decision trees [30], which is a random subset of the training data. The test object's final class is chosen to be one that aggregates votes from the various decision trees.

- SVM

SVM models are a type of supervised learning method that may be used for both classification and regression issues, but is most frequently used for classification problems. This classifier is a widely used statistical model that is built on a logistic function applied to a binary dependent variable in the model [31].

- Decision Tree

A decision tree is a tree structure that resembles a flowchart. It is a method for classification and prediction that uses nodes and inter-nodes to describe the data. The root and internal nodes are test cases that are used to distinguish instances with varying characteristics. Internal nodes are generated as a result of attribute testing. The class variable is denoted by the leaf nodes [32].

- Linear Regression

Logistic regression is a technique for binary classification. The input variables are expected to be numeric and to have a Gaussian distribution. It is not required for the last statement to be true in logistic regression. In other words, the method is capable of producing acceptable results even when the data is not Gaussian. Each input value is assigned a coefficient, which is then linearly merged into a regression function and converted using a logistic function [33].

4 Evaluation & Result

In this part, the results of implemented performance measurements are shown using the Orange toolkit's pleasant graphical interface.

4.1 Setup of Experiments with Results

This subpart explains the procedure of sampling used, the parameters of the classification model, and the CM for every algorithm.

- Method of Sampling

The developed models' performance is evaluated using a K-fold cross-validation sampling approach [27]. The whole datasets are cross-validated tenfold in this article (2000 records). The data were divided into tenfold samples. The classification model is trained on seven folds, with the remaining fold serving as a testing set. As a result, for training the model 70% and for testing the model 30% of data records were utilized.

- Decision Tree

The CM of the Tree classifier is demonstrated in Fig. 3. Out of 500 data points, which are labeled as '0', the correct classification is for 402 records. Out of 268 data points, which are labeled as '1', the correct classification is for 142 records.

The Confusion matrix illustrates four critical metrics for evaluating the Decision Tree Classifier model: true positive (TP), true negative (TN), false positive (FP), and false negative (FN). Where TP = 142, TN = 402, FP 126 and FN = 98.

- SVM

To learn the model, the attribute space is transformed into a new feature space using a Radial Basis Function (RBF) kernel. The maximum number of iterations authorized was 100. Figure 4 depicts the SVM classifier's confusion matrix.

Whereas out of 500 data points, which are labeled as '0', the correct classification is for 401 records and out of 268 data points, which are labeled as '1', the correct classification is for 152 records. Again, the values of four critical metrics are TP = 152, TN = 401, FP = 116, and FN = 99.

- KNN

Figure 5 illustrates the KNN classifier's confusion matrix. The nearest neighbours' numbers was set to five in the KNN model, and the usage of Euclidean distance was done to calculate the distance between two points, with points weighted according to their distance from the query point.

We can see in Fig. 5, The CM summarizes four critical metrics for evaluating the KNN Where TP = 156, TN = 413, FP = 112 and FN = 87.

- Random Forest

A forest was incorporated here with 10 decision trees. In Fig. 6, the model's confusion matrix is depicted. The CM illustrates four critical metrics for evaluating the Decision Tree Classifier model, where TP = 161, TN = 425, FP = 107, and FN = 75.

• Naive Bayes

Whereas out of 500 data points, which are labeled as '0', the correct classification is for 403 records and out of 268 data points, which are labeled as '1', the correct and successful classification is for 182 records.

The CM illustrates four critical metrics for evaluating the Naive Bayes Classifier model, where TP = 182 TN = 403, FP = 86 and FN = 97.

• Artificial Neural Network

In this model, back-propagation was applied with a multi-layer perceptron (MLP) approach. Each buried layer had 200 neurons with a Rectified Linear Unit (ReLu) activation function. The Adam technique was then employed to efficiently optimise stochastic weights. In Fig. 8, the con-fusion matrix for the neural network model is shown. Whereas out of 500 data points, which are labeled as '0', the correct classification is for 431 records and out of 268 data points, which are labeled as '1', the correct classification is for 157 records. The Confusion matrix summarizes four critical metrics for evaluating an ANN Classifier model as TP = 157, TN = 431, FP = 111, and FN = 69.

• Logistic Regression

This model's regularization is set to ridges (L2), and the cost strength is set to its default value of one (C = 1). The model's CM is depicted in Fig. 9.

From 500 data points labeled 0, 442 records were successfully identified, while from 268 data points labeled 1, 151 records were correctly classified.

True positive (TP), true negative (TN), false positive (FP), and false negative (FN) are four significant metrics used to assess Logistic Regression Classifier model (FN). TP = 151, TN = 442; FP = 117; FN = 58 (Fig. 7).

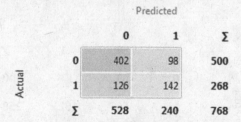

Fig. 3. CM of tree classifier

• Comparison of Performance

The classification methods performance on the dataset of diabetes is examined and compared. The following sections contain details on performance measurements and comparisons.

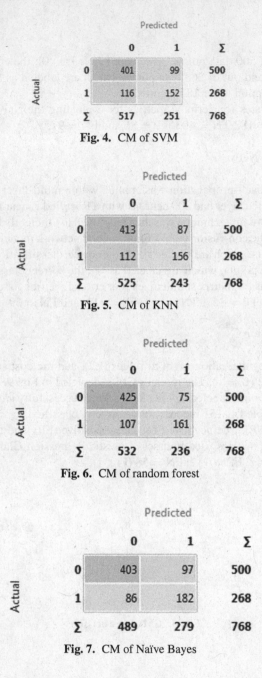

Actual \ Predicted	0	1	Σ
0	401	99	500
1	116	152	268
Σ	517	251	768

Fig. 4. CM of SVM

Actual \ Predicted	0	1	Σ
0	413	87	500
1	112	156	268
Σ	525	243	768

Fig. 5. CM of KNN

Actual \ Predicted	0	1	Σ
0	425	75	500
1	107	161	268
Σ	532	236	768

Fig. 6. CM of random forest

Actual \ Predicted	0	1	Σ
0	403	97	500
1	86	182	268
Σ	489	279	768

Fig. 7. CM of Naïve Bayes

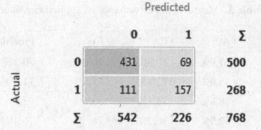

Fig. 8. CM of artificial neural network

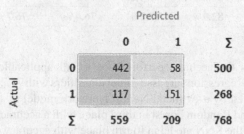

Fig. 9. CM of logistic regression

- **Evaluation Measures of Performance**

As mentioned before, the CM illustrates four critical metrics for evaluating classification models: true negative (TN), true positive (TP), false negative (FN) and false positive (FP). These metrics are applied to calculate the following measures of performance:

a) Recall b) Precision c) Accuracy D) F1-measure. These performance metrics are derived by the use of (TP, TN, FP, and FN). The following metrics are used in this study to examine and evaluate categorization models:

$$Accuracy = \frac{TP + TN}{TP + TN + FP + FN} \tag{1}$$

$$precision = \frac{TP}{TP + FP} \tag{2}$$

$$Re\ call = \frac{TP}{TP = FN} \tag{3}$$

$$F1 - measure = \frac{2 \times (precision \times recall)}{precision + recall} \tag{4}$$

- **Classification Model Comparison**

The performance of the implemented classifiers is assessed in this subsection using the aforementioned metrics. Table 3 summarizes the performance metrics for the classifiers used.

Table 3. Measures of performance of applied classifiers

Method	AUC	CA	F1	Precision	Recall
Tree	67.9%	70.8%	70.04%	70.2%	70.8%
SVM	75.9%	72%	71.8%	71.6%	72.0%
KNN	78.8%	74.1%	73.8%	73.6%	74.1%
Naïve Bayes	82.9%	76.2%	76.3%	76.4%	76.2%
Random Forest	81.1%	76.3%	75.9%	75.8%	76.3%
Neural Network	82.6%	76.6%	76%	76.0%	76.6%
Logistic Regression	**82.9%**	**77.2%**	**76.4%**	**76.7%**	**77.2%**

It also compares the accurate performance of all applicable models. It is self-evident that Logistic Regression surpasses other classifiers with 77.2% accuracy. Logistic Regression is followed by a Artificial Neural Network model in second place with an accuracy of 76.6% and Random Forest in third place with a accuracy of 76.3%. Random forest is followed by the KNN model in fourth place with accuracy of 74.1%. And SVM got fifth position with accuracy of 72%. Decision tree with the accuracy of 70.8% is the worst case. Logistic regression outperforms in all performance measures like AUC, F1-score, Precision and Recall, which can be shown in Table 3.

5   Conclusion

Automatic diabetes detection is a significant real-world medical issue. Early detection and management of diabetes are critical. This article demonstrates the use of several classifiers, including Decision Trees, SVM, KNN, Naive Bayes, Random Forest, Neural Network, and Logistic Regression, to simulate actual diabetes diagnosis for local and systemic therapy, as well as presenting relevant work in the field and the outcome indicates that Logistic Regression outperforms all other classifiers. The suggested model's usefulness is demonstrated by experimental data. The performance of the strategies was evaluated in relation to the problem of diabetes diagnosis. Experiments validate the given model. In the future, it is planned to compile data from several locations across India and develop a more precise and broad predictive model for diabetes diagnosis. Future research will similarly focus on accumulating data from a later time period and identifying additional possible prognostic factors to integrate. The technique might be expanded and refined to automate the analysis of diabetes.

References

1. https://www.who.int/news-room/fact-sheets/detail/diabetes
2. Amin, D.M., Garg, A.: Performance analysis of data mining algorithms. J. Comput. Theor. Nanosci. **16**(9), 3849–3853 (2019). https://doi.org/10.1166/jctn.2019.8260

3. Saichanma, S., Chulsomlee, S., Thangrua, N., Pongsuchart, P., Sanmun, D.: The observation report of red blood cell morphology in Thailand teenager by using data mining technique. Adv. Hematol. **2014**, 1–5 (2014). https://doi.org/10.1155/2014/493706
4. Canlas, R.D. (2009). Data Mining in Healthcare: Current applications & Issues, Unpublished Master Thesis, 1–10
5. Iyer, A., Jeyalatha, S., Sumbaly, R.: Diagnosis of diabetes using classification mining techniques. Int. J. Data Min. Knowl. Manag. Process **5**(1), 01–14 (2015). https://doi.org/10.5121/ijdkp.2015.5101
6. Aljumah, A.A., Ahamad, M.G., Siddiqui, M.K.: Application of data mining: diabetes health care in young and old patients. Journal of King Saud University - Computer and Information Sciences **25**(2), 127–136 (2013). https://doi.org/10.1016/j.jksuci.2012.10.003
7. Barakat, N., Bradley, A.P., Barakat, M.N.H.: Intelligible support vector machines for diagnosis of diabetes mellitus. IEEE Trans. Inf. Technol. Biomed. **14**(4), 1114–1120 (2010). https://doi.org/10.1109/titb.2009.2039485
8. Komi, M., Li, J., Zhai, Y., Zhang, X.: Application of data mining methods in diabetes prediction. In: 2nd International Conference on Image, Vision and Computing (ICIVC), pp. 1006–1010 (2017)
9. Pradeep, K.R., Naveen, N.C.: Predictive analysis of diabetes using J48 algorithm of classification techniques. In: 2nd International Conference on Contemporary Computing and Informatics (IC3I), pp. 347–352 (2016)
10. Kavakiotis, I., Tsave, O., Salifoglou, A., Maglaveras, N., Vlahavas, I., Chouvarda, I.: Machine learning and data mining methods in diabetes research. Comput. Struct. Biotechnol. J. **15**, 104–116 (2017). https://doi.org/10.1016/j.csbj.2016.12.005
11. Nilashi, M., Ibrahim, O.B., Ahmadi, H., Shahmoradi, L.: An analytical method for diseases prediction using machine learning techniques. Comput. Chem. Eng. **106**, 212–223 (2017). https://doi.org/10.1016/j.compchemeng.2017.06.011
12. Kamadi, V.V., Allam, A.R., Thummala, S.M.: A computational intelligence technique for the effective diagnosis of diabetic patients using principal component analysis (PCA) and modified fuzzy SLIQ decision tree approach. Appl. Soft Comput. **49**, 137–145 (2016). https://doi.org/10.1016/j.asoc.2016.05.010
13. Perveen, S., Shahbaz, M., Guergachi, A., Keshavjee, K.: Performance analysis of data mining classification techniques to predict diabetes. Procedia Comput. Sci. **82**, 115–121 (2016). https://doi.org/10.1016/j.procs.2016.04.016
14. Rathore, A., Chauhan, S., Gujral, S.: Detecting and predicting diabetes using supervised learning: an approach towards better healthcare for women. Int. J. Adv. Res. Comput. Sci. **8**(5), 1192–1195 (2017)
15. Mahmud, S.M.H., et al.: Machine Learning Based Unified Framework for Diabetes Prediction. Association for Computing Machinery. China (2018). https://doi.org/10.1145/3297730.3297737
16. Ahuja, R., Sharma, S.C., Ali, M.: A diabetic disease prediction model based on classification algorithms. Annals of Emerging Technologies in Computing **3**(3), 44–52 (2019). https://doi.org/10.33166/aetic.2019.03.005
17. García-Ordás, M.T., Benavides, C., Benítez-Andrades, J.A., Alaiz-Moretón, H., García-Rodríguez, I.: Diabetes detection using deep learning techniques with oversampling and feature augmentation. Comput. Methods Programs Biomed. **202**, 105968 (2021). https://doi.org/10.1016/j.cmpb.2021.105968
18. Bukhari, M.M., Alkhamees, B.F., Hussain, S., Gumaei, A., Assiri, A., Ullah, S.S.: An improved artificial neural network model for effective diabetes prediction. Complexity **2021**, 1–10 (2021). https://doi.org/10.1155/2021/5525271

19. Roy, K., et al.: An enhanced machine learning framework for type 2 diabetes classification using imbalanced data with missing values. Complexity **2021**, 1–21 (2021). https://doi.org/10.1155/2021/9953314

20. Khanam, J.J., Foo, S.Y.: A comparison of machine learning algorithms for diabetes prediction. ICT Express **7**(4), 432–439 (2021). https://doi.org/10.1016/j.icte.2021.02.004

21. Orange – Data Mining Fruitful & Fun. https://orange.biolab.si/

22. Diabetes –dataset. https://www.kaggle.com/datasets/uciml/pima-indians-diabetes-database/. Accessed 01 April 2022

23. Pattnaik, P.K., Rautaray, S.S., Das, H., Nayak, J.: Progress in computing, analytics and networking. In: Proceedings of ICCAN 2017 (2018)

24. Garcia, S., Luengo, J., Herra, F.: Data Preprocessing in Data Mining. Springer (2015). https://doi.org/10.1007/978-3-319-10247-4

25. Alsalamah, M., Amin, S., Palade, V.: Clinical practice for diagnostic causes for obstructive sleep apnea using artificial intelligent neural networks. In: Miraz, M.H., Excell, P., Ware, A., Soomro, S., Ali, M. (eds.) iCETiC 2018. LNICSSITE, vol. 200, pp. 259–272. Springer, Cham (2018). https://doi.org/10.1007/978-3-319-95450-9_22

26. Witten, I.H., Frank, E., Hall, M.A., Pal, C.J.: Data Mining: Practical Machine Learning Tools and Techniques. Morgan Kaufmann (2016)

27. Rennie, J.D., et al.: Tackling the poor asumptions of naive bayes text classifiers. In: Proceedings of the 20th International Conference on Machine Learning (ICML 2003), pp. 616–623 (2003)

28. Chen, G.H., Shah, D.: Explaining the success of nearest neighbor methods in prediction. Found. Trends® Mach. Learn. **10**(5–6), 337–588 (2018). https://doi.org/10.1561/2200000064

29. van Gerven, M., Bohte, S.: Artificial neural networks as models of neural information processing. Front. Comput. Neurosci. **11**, 114 (2017). https://doi.org/10.3389/fncom.2017.00114

30. Davies, A., Ghahramani, Z.: The random forest kernal and other kiernals for big data from random partitions (2014). arXiv.1402.4293

31. Smola, A.J., Schölkopf, B.: A tutorial on support vector regression. Stat. Comput. **14**(3), 199–222 (2004). https://doi.org/10.1023/b:stco.0000035301.49549.88

32. Rokach, L.: Data Mining with Decision Trees: Theory and Application, vol. 81. World Scientific (2014)

33. Weisberg, S.: Applied Linear Regression, 4th ed. Wiley (2013)

Networks, Security and Privacy Parallel and Distributed Networks

Prediction of DDoS Attacks Using Machine Learning Algorithms Based on Classification Technique

Anupama Mishra[1][(✉)] and Deepesh Rawat[2]

[1] Computer Science and Engineering, Himalayan School of Science and Technology, Swami Rama Himalayan University, Dehradun, India
anupamamishra@srhu.edu.in
[2] Electronics & Communication Engineering, Himalayan School of Science and Technology, Swami Rama Himalayan University, Dehradun, India

Abstract. Distributed denial of service attacks often know as network threat is a severe threat, and are a type of cyber-attack that are directed at a particular system or network in an effort to make that system or net-work out of reach and unusable for a period of time. The improved detection of a wide variety of dis-tributed denial-of-service (DDoS) cyber threats by utilizing advanced algorithms and a higher level of accuracy while maintaining a manageable level of computational cost has consequently emerged as the utmost essential part of detecting DDoS in today's world. The DDoS attack that has been launched against the targeted network or system must be determined in view of defending the machines in a net-work that has been targeted. In this paper, a number of ensemble classification techniques are dis-cussed, which combine the performance of various algorithms to improve overall performance. Using many performance metrics such as a receiver operating characteristics (ROC) curves, precision, accuracy, recall and F1 scores, we present and analyzed the performance of algorithms used in our proposed approach.

Keywords: Distributed denial of service attack · Machine learning · Random forest · Naïve Bayes · Decision tree

1 Introduction

A denial-of-service attack, according to the World Wide Web security question, is one that is "de-signed to prevent a computer or network from providing normal services [1]." The rapid expansion of Internet has resulted the specific type of DoS attack development that has proven to be extremely effective and difficult to defend against the distributed DoS attack. This attacks do not originate from a single source, but rather from a number of spoofed sources that use a variety of attack types in a coordinated effort. Fake Internet Protocol (IP) addresses, as opposed to real ones, are used to identify computers that are either unwitting accomplices or that the attacker has control over. Attackers are able to coordinate deadly attacks on multiple targets at the same time using their own resources

© The Author(s), under exclusive license to Springer Nature Switzerland AG 2022
R. Mehra et al. (Eds.): ICCISC 2022, CCIS 1672, pp. 39–50, 2022.
https://doi.org/10.1007/978-3-031-22915-2_4

and the resources of their "zombies," resulting in greater damage in a shorter amount of time than they could have done otherwise [2].

A distributed denial of service which is also a cyberattack can bring websites, servers, and other online services to a crawl. The perpetrator uses multiple computers and devices to send fraudulent requests to a server, making it appear that the server is being attacked by a large number of people. The term is some-times used interchangeably with the term "denial of service attack", but "DDOS" refers specifically to an attack that uses multiple sources to flood a target with requests. Some DDOS attacks involve the use of botnets, which are networks of compromised computers and devices that have been malware-infected without the users' knowledge [3].

DDoS is a form of cyberattack where a network is attacked with heavy traffic that's create a problem for users to access a website or service. This type of attack is often used as a tactic to make a target site or service appear overwhelmed or unreliable to users. DDoS attacks can also be used to force a website or service to a user to a specific location, where it is under the control of the attacker. DDoS attacks are often used for online harassment, for example, when a website is under constant attack and can't improve its performance or stay online [4]. DDoS is a method of disrupting a system in a network by sending a large amount of data to a server or system from multiple different sources. The result is that the system or network is not able to handle the load and ultimately crashes. This makes the system or net-work unavailable to its intended use [5].

DDoS is a form of cyberattack where multiple hosts are used to bombard a web server or other net-work target with data, often using a botnet or other network of malware-infected computers, until the target's resources are consumed and it is rendered inaccessible to legitimate users. Unlike a traditional DoS attack, where a single host is used to flood a target's resources and crash their services, a DDoS at-tack is much more complicated and powerful. DDoS attacks can be extremely difficult to stop due to their decentralized nature. DDoS attacks can be carried out with a handful of hosts or even a single host, making them much more difficult to detect and investigate [6]. A denial of service refers to a situation in which a service or resource is utilized to the point of being rendered unusable or inaccessible to other users. These are often seen in the context of online gaming servers, but can also affect online banking or shopping services.

A distributed denial of service occurs when a single device or user is able to bring down a server or network resource. This can be accomplished by distributing a request across a network, such as when a single computer is used to send an entire file to a website. Figure 1 depicts how this attack [3] had a significant impact on the telecommunications industry [7]. Current and former employees of several tech companies are accusing Amazon, Facebook, Google and Microsoft of failing to protect their employees from the COVID-19 pandemic, with some accusing the companies of endangering their workers' safety. We've seen this story before. In the wake of a string of high-profile layoffs, employees have accused the companies of not doing enough to protect their workers' health. But for companies as large as Amazon and Facebook, the risks of a pandemic are remote. Therefore, the developed technology helps in this field to defend our system and network from the threat. Machine learning is one of the technologies which is being used for defensive mechanisms in many applications.

Following are the sections that provides an outline for the paper: Sect. 2 presents the related work based on existing defensive mechanisms, our proposed work is discussed in Sect. 3. Section 4 evaluated the research work, and Sect. 5 brings the research to its conclusion.

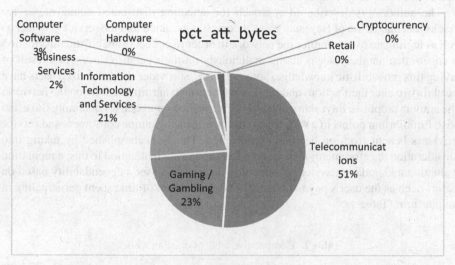

Fig. 1. Impact of distributed denial of service attacks

2 Related Work

Machine learning allows to compare models with different features, which can help to choose the one that is best for the use of applications. Specifically, we can use a machine learning model to identify which types of data are most predictive of the outcome of interest, such as cyberattack.

A defensive approach based on low-cost was proposed by the authors in [6, 7]and focused in calculation of the entropy between benign traffic and DDoS attacks. As an additional suggestion, the authors Intensity reduction strategy for dealing with attacks has the following characteristics: The following are three advantages of using this methodology over other current methods: The first is that it has a high level of detection. In addition to having a reduces false alarm, also the capability of detecting small changes in the environment at a rapid pace along with the mitigate approach.

The authors [7] developed a solution for resolving authentication and security challenges connected to smart vessels in sea transport. An identity-based approach is used to authenticate the access for smart vessel and devices. But the method is limited to maritime transportation.

An auction with many attributes was proposed in [8] to mitigate distributed DDoS attacks on a net-work. A reputation-based detection approach was proposed, in which the minimal utility defines the user's reputation. A payment plan for normal users and another for fraudulent users, as well as an identifying mechanism are proposed in addition with the identification method. In this method, a greedy re-source for allocation strategy is used to ensure that resources are distributed appropriately among legitimate users. Differential payment systems are designed to penalize malevolent users that manipulate their offers in order to obtain the maximum possible share of limited resources.

The authors [9] describe an approach for detecting distributed denial of service attacks that makes use of Bayesian game theory. It is assumed that the service provider as well as legitimate users monitor the network in order to collect probabilistic information to ensure that another user is acting maliciously on their behalf or not. As a result of having this probabilistic knowledge, both the service provider and authorized users have the ability to alter their actions and replies in reaction to harmful activity on the network. The authors propose a Bayesian pricing [10] and auction approach for obtaining Bayesian Nash Equilibrium points in a variety of settings in which genuine consumers and service providers benefit from probabilistic knowledge. This is accomplished by taking into consideration the aforementioned assumptions and facts. In addition to this, a reputation evaluation and updating system is offered to determine a user's dependability based on factors such as the user's payment history and the amount of time spent participating in the platform (Table 1).

Table 1. Comparative table of existing work.

References	Techniques	Merits	Limitation
[10]	Used SDN (Software Defined Network	Detection Rate is high	Only work on Volume based DDoS
[11]	Worked on IBE (Identity Based Encryption)	Detection Rate is high	Overhead is high
[12]	Worked on IBS (Identity Based Signature) along with IBE	Detection rate is moderate	Overhead is high
[13]	Based on Boosting Algorithms	Detection rate is moderate	False alarms

3 Proposed Work

3.1 Approach

In our paper, we are primarily concerned with data preprocessing, selection of significant features [13], machine modelling through a classifier, and then finally prediction on testing dataset. After performance evaluation on results, the research work is concluded. The approach includes the following activities [14–19]:

Preparation of information: This phase is concerned with preparation of the data which is comprised of tasks helps on processing the raw data into a clean dataset.

If the raw data is not in a usable state at the time of completion, the type and order of activities may change, and Some of the unrelatable features may be removed. A few examples of the responsibilities involved are data cleansing, feature selection, and data transformation. In our work, Fig. 2 depicts the best 15 features by using extra tree classifiers. The selected features are: ACK Flag Count, Inbound, URG Flag Count, Destination IP, Source IP, Init_Win_bytes_forward, Timestamp, Flow ID, Pro-tocol, Min Packet Length, min_seg_size_forward, Destination Port, Max Packet Length, Average Packet Size, and Packet Length Std.

Modelling: In the modelling phase, modelling techniques are applied to the data. This is done in order to achieve the best possible performance by adjusting the parameters of the models in question.

As previously indicated, this step is closely tied to data preparation because modelling might disclose previously unknown data errors. Depending on the situation, the data preparation method can result in the employment of several models.

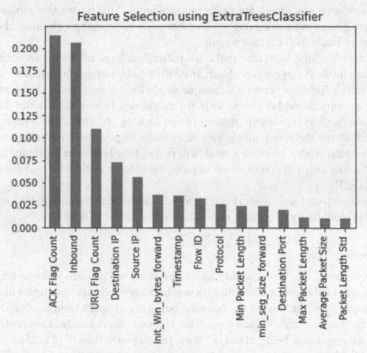

Fig. 2. 15 Best Features are selected by using extra trees classifiers

3.2 Modelling

In order to compare and contrast the datasets, three different supervised learning classifiers are selected based on a number of parameters [15–17], including the parametric models and nonparametric models, applications and use of algorithms have been discussed and used in previous work.

3.2.1 Random Forest

A machine learning algorithm that is used to classify a dataset into a specific category. It is a combination of many decision trees. The results of the decision trees are combined in a way that helps reduce the error rate of the classification. This is similar to how a forest is grown [20–22].

Random forest is a machine learning technique that groups examples together by their similarity, rather than grouping them by their distance to the target classification. This is often referred to as "many small decisions," as opposed to "one big decision," which is how other machine learning techniques work. This means that random forest will, on average, get more things right than other machine learning techniques. However, it is also more likely to get things wrong.

A machine learning technique that finds patterns in large numbers of variables. For example, in a medical diagnosis problem, instead of just looking at a patient's symptoms and lab results, a machine learning technique might look at millions of different combinations of symptoms and lab results to find patterns that help make a better diagnosis. In a financial prediction problem, instead of just looking at a stock's past performance, a machine learning technique might look at millions of past stock trans-actions to find patterns that help predict whether a stock will rise or fall. The same is true for any other problem: finding the right combination of input variables is critical for making accurate predictions [23].

The random forest technique is often more effective than traditional decision trees, because it is more likely to capture non-linear relationships in data.

3.2.2 Decision Tree

Decision trees are a machine learning technique that finds patterns in large amounts of data. In a traditional decision tree, the data is split into two groups: examples that should be classified as "yes" or "no" in the question being asked, and examples that should be classified as "yes" or "no" on their own. This is a two-class classification problem. For example, if the question being asked is "does this dog have fleas?" [24, 25].

A machine learning technique that uses decision trees to make a classification. Each decision tree is built on a subset of the original data. The random forest technique is often more effective than traditional decision trees, because it is more likely to capture non-linear relationships in data. Data is split into a number of groups, and each group is given a separate decision tree.

A machine learning technique that finds patterns in large numbers of variables. For example, in a medical diagnosis problem, instead of just looking at a patient's symptoms and lab results, a machine learning technique might look at millions of different combinations of symptoms and lab results to find pat-terns that help make a better diagnosis.

In a financial prediction problem, instead of just looking at a stock's past performance, a machine learning technique might look at millions of past stock transactions to find patterns that help predict whether a stock will rise or fall. The same is true for any other problem: finding the right combination of input variables is critical for making accurate predictions. It is a tree-based method that uses the outcome of a single decision tree as the input for the next tree in the forest. This helps reduce the error rate of the classification. This is similar to how a forest is grown [26].

Decision trees are one of the most basic machine learning techniques. They are a machine learning technique that finds patterns in large numbers of input variables. To build a decision tree, a machine learning technique starts by choosing a subset of the original data as the root node and then from there, the machine learning technique divides the original data into subsets, or nodes, based on some criteria, such as variable type or variable range.

3.2.3 Naïve Bayes

A machine learning technique that uses Bayes theorem to make predictions. The Naive Bayes ma-chine learning technique assumes that each input variable is independent of the others. For example, if a machine learning technique is trying to predict whether a person has a certain disease, Naive Bayes would assume that the presence or absence of a symptom has no effect on the prediction. This assumption turns out to be surprisingly accurate in many cases [27, 28].

An example of a machine learning technique that uses decision trees is the naïve Bayes classification machine learning technique and often used in text classification problems. In a text classification problem, the naïve Bayes machine learning technique uses decision trees to classify text into different categories. The naïve Bayes machine learning technique uses decision trees instead of other machine learning techniques because decision trees are able to capture non-linear relationships in data better than other machine learning techniques.

Naive Bayes [18, 19] used to make predictions. It is often one of the first machine learning techniques that people learn because it is easy to understand. The Naive Bayes machine learning technique is also often used as a simple baseline to compare the accuracy of other machine learning techniques. For ex-ample, if a machine learning technique is twice as accurate as the Naive Bayes machine learning technique, then it is likely that the first machine learning technique is a good one.

Naive Bayes is a machine learning technique that is used to make a prediction. It is a classification technique. For example, if the question being asked is "Will it rain today? a Naive Bayes technique might be used to predict whether it will rain today. It is a machine learning technique that finds patterns in large numbers of variables. It works on bayes theorem by combining the probability that a certain in-put will lead to a certain output with the probability that a different input will lead to the same output.

4 Result Analysis

We have the following metrics for evaluating the performance of classification machine learning [29–31]. Performance metrics for machine learning such as precision, recall, and f1-score are used to evaluate the quality of the model. These metrics can be used to compare the performance of different models and to evaluate the impact of different training regimes on model performance. Precision is a measure of the number of correctly classified examples. It is calculated as the ratio of the number of examples correctly classified by the model to the total number of examples in the training set.

The precision is the percentage of the time that an output was actually produced. The recall is the per-centage of the time that a specific output was actually identified. Table 2, Fig. 3 and 4 are used to show the results as precision, recall , f1 score and accuracy.

Table 2. Classification report of applied algorithms.

	Decision Tree			Random Forest			Naïve Bayes		
	Precision	Recall	F1 Score	Precision	Recall	F1 Score	Precision	Recall	F1 Score
Benign	94	98	96	94	100	97	84	100	94
DDoS	100	100	100	100	100	100	100	99	100

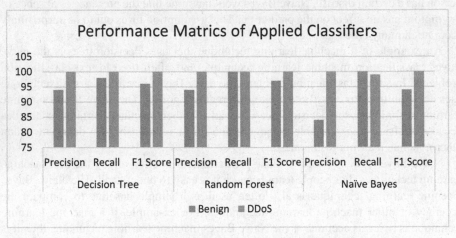

Fig. 3. Performance metrics of applied classifiers

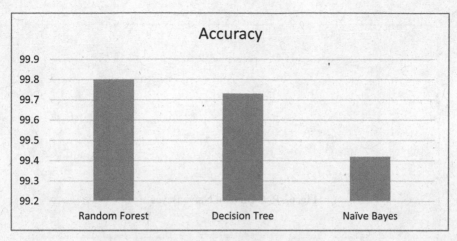

Fig. 4. Accuracy of applied classifiers

As shown in Figs. 5, 6 and 7, the results are discussed and analyzed. All three of them performed admirably when it came to classifying DDoS traffic. The results of the performance metric evaluations can be confirmed through the examination of the RoC Curve.

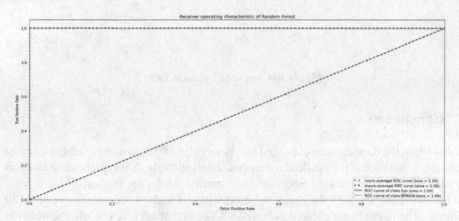

Fig. 5. RoC curve of Random Forest

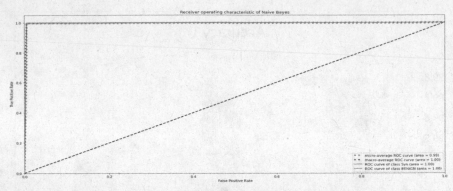

Fig. 6. RoC curve of Naïve Bayes

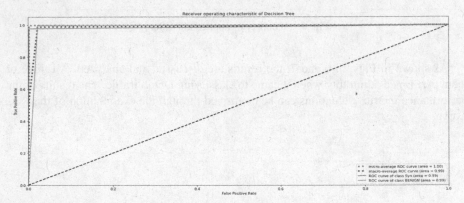

Fig. 7. RoC curve of Decision Tree

5   Conclusion

In this study, the datasets were classified into binary classification using machine learning classifiers, and each class was detected and validated properly. A comprehensive analysis of multiple machine learning algorithms was carried out for the purpose of identifying DDoS cyber threats, with the Random Forest with the highest accuracy score of 99.80 percent. The naive bayes method achieved 99.42 percent accuracy, while the decision tree achieved 99.75 percent accuracy in achieving the target. For future work, types of DDoS attacks can be targeted for classification and prediction in the future.

References

1. Badve, O.P., et al.: Taxonomy of DoS and DDoS attacks and desirable defense mechanism in a cloud computing environment. Neural Comput. Appl. **28**(12), 3655–3682 (2017)
2. Gupta, B.B., et al.: A comprehensive survey on DDoS attacks and recent defense mechanisms. In: Handbook of Research on Intrusion Detection Systems, pp. 186–218. IGI Global (2020)
3. https://radar.cloudflare.com/notebooks/ddos-2022-q1. Accessed 2 Apr 2022

4. Mishra, A., et al.: Security threats and recent countermeasures in cloud computing. Modern Principles, Practices, and Algorithms for Cloud Security, pp. 145–161. IGI Global (2020)
5. Mishra, A., Gupta, N.: Analysis of Cloud Computing Vulnerability against DDoS. In: International Conference on Innovative Sustainable Computational Technologies (CISCT), pp. 1–6. IEEE (2019)
6. Mishra, A., Gupta, N., Gupta, B.B.: Defense mechanisms against DDoS attack based on entropy in SDN-cloud using POX controller. Telecommun. Syst. **77**(1), 47–62 (2021). https://doi.org/10.1007/s11235-020-00747-w
7. Gaurav, A., et al.: Identity-based authentication mechanism for secure information sharing in the mari-time transport system. IEEE Trans. Intell. Transp. Syst. (2021)
8. Nguyen, G.N., et al.: Secure blockchain enabled cyber–physical systems in healthcare using deep belief network with ResNet model. J. Parallel Distrib. Comput. **153**, 150–160 (2021)
9. Zhou, Z., et al.: A fine-grained access control and security approach for intelligent vehicular transport in 6g communication system. IEEE Trans. Intell. Transp. Syst. (2021)
10. Dahiya, A., Gupta, B.B.: Multi attribute auction based incentivized solution against DDoS attacks. Comput. Secur. **92**, 101763 (2020)
11. Cvitić, I., et al.: Boosting-based DDoS detection in internet of things systems. IEEE Internet of Things J. **9**, 2109–2123 (2021)
12. Dahiya, A., et al.: A reputation score policy and Bayesian game theory based incentivised mechanism for DDoS attacks mitigation and cyber defense. Future Generation Computer Systems (2020)
13. Han, J., et al.: Data Mining: Concepts and Techniques. Elsevier (2011)
14. DDoS 2019 | Datasets | Research | Canadian Institute for Cybersecurity | UNB. Accessed 28 Apr 2022
15. Alzahrani, R.J., et al.: Security analysis of DDoS attacks using machine learning algorithms in networks traffic. Electronics **10**(23), 2919 (2021)
16. He, Z., Zhang, T., Lee, R.B.: Machine learning based DDoS attack detection from source side in cloud. In: Proceedings of the 2017 IEEE 4th International Conference on Cyber Security and Cloud Computing (CSCloud), New York, NY, USA, 26–28 June 2017, pp. 114–120 (2017)
17. Aamir, M., et al.: DDoS attack detection with feature engineering and machine learning: the framework and performance evaluation. Int. J. Inf. Secur. **18**, 761–785 (2019)
18. Liu, Z., et al.: The prediction of DDoS attack by machine learning. In: Third International Conference on Electronics and Communication; Network and Computer Technology (ECNCT 2021), vol. 12167, pp. 681–686. SPIE (2022)
19. Zewdie, T.G., Girma, A.: An evaluation framework for machine learning methods in detection of DoS and DDoS intrusion. In: 2022 International Conference on Artificial Intelligence in Information and Communication (ICAIIC), pp. 115–121 (2022)
20. Sahoo, S., et al.: Multiple features based approach for automatic fake news detection on social net-works using deep learning. Appl. Soft Comput. **100**, 106983 (2021)
21. Cvitić, I., Peraković, D., Periša, M., Gupta, B.: Ensemble machine learning approach for classification of IoT devices in smart home. Int. J. Mach. Learn. Cybern. **12**(11), 3179–3202 (2021). https://doi.org/10.1007/s13042-020-01241-0
22. Gupta, B.B., et al.: Machine learning and smart card based two-factor authentication scheme for pre-serving anonymity in telecare medical information system (TMIS). Neural Computing and Applications, 1–26 (2021). https://doi.org/10.1007/s00521-021-06152-x
23. Yamaguchi, S., Gupta, B.: Malware threat in Internet of Things and its mitigation analysis. In: Research Anthology on Combating Denial-of-Service Attacks, pp. 371–387. IGI Global (2021)

24. Peraković, D., et al.: A Big Data and Deep Learning based Approach for DDoS Detection in Cloud Computing Environment. In: 2021 IEEE 10th Global Conference on Consumer Electronics (GCCE), pp. 287–290. IEEE (2021)

25. Dahiya, A., et al.: A PBNM and economic incentive-based defensive mechanism against DDoS at-tacks. Enterp. Inf. Syst. **16**(3), 406–426 (2022)

26. Dahiya, A., et al.: A reputation score policy and Bayesian game theory based incentivized mechanism for DDoS attacks mitigation and cyber defense. Futur. Gener. Comput. Syst. **117**, 193–204 (2021)

27. Chartuni, A., et al.: Multi-classifier of DDoS attacks in computer networks built on neural networks. Appl. Sci. **11**(22), 10609 (2021)

28. Zhu, X., et al.: Prediction of rockhead using a hybrid N-XGBoost machine learning framework. J. Rock Mech. Geotech. Eng. **13**(6), 1231–1245 (2021)

29. Teles, G., Rodrigues, J.J., Rabêlo, R.A., Kozlov, S.A.: Comparative study of support vector machines and random forests machine learning algorithms on credit operation. Software: Practice and Experience **51**(12), 2492–2500 (2021)

30. Gaurav, A., et al.: A comprehensive survey on machine learning approaches for malware detection in IoT-based enterprise information system. Enterprise Information Systems, 1–25 (2022)

31. Pedregosa, F., et al.: Scikit-learn: machine learning in python. J. Mach. Learn. Res. **12**, 2825–2830 (2011)

Role of Internet of Things and Cloud Computing in Education System: A Review

Ajay Krishan Gairola[1,2](✉) and Vidit Kumar[1] (iD)

[1] Graphic Era Deemed to Be University, Dehradun, India
ajaykrishangairola@gmail.com
[2] Graphic Era Hill University, Dehradun, India

Abstract. The current outbreak of the coronavirus (COVID19) pandemic has affected education across the world. To meet the current challenges posed by COVID19, educational institutions (schools, colleges and universities) need to be more efficient in providing quality educational services virtually. Cloud computing and Internet of things (IOT) are such technologies that accomplishes this. In this work, we review the recent works related to the cloud technology and IOT in education system and explores its various benefits and challenges. Furthermore, this article examines recent work on the potential scope of IoT in the Education Sector.

Keywords: Cloud computing · Virtual learning · Internet of Things · Online teaching · Virtual classes · Smart device

1 Introduction

The international quarantine imposed since December 2019 due to the coronavirus pandemic has put pressure on us to reconsider the idea of e-learning [1]. Cloud computing is a must-have within the academic process, and it is widely employed in enterprises. For individuals in every aspect of the process of mastery, cloud technology makes training a true and enjoyable pleasure. With the help of smart devices, students can now communicate with each other or with teachers and experience the flexibility of learning. The offerings of cloud computing have advanced the results of an institution's study and have allowed professors and college students to access this modern technology as well as receive additional blessings. Over time the educational system has changed and at the same time is no longer limited to blackboard classrooms and textbooks. Training in the cutting edge landscape of cloud computing has emerged as an advantage for the commercial enterprise, while all and sundry are trying their hardest to combat the virus posed by COVID-19 [18]. From preserving scholarly data to storing information, from online training systems to advanced study analysis, it has completely revolutionized teaching-learning training. Students, professors, and instructors can now enjoy cloud-primarily based totally training's accessibility and convenience. The Internet of Things connects processes, people, data, and devices, making it easier for education stakeholders to convert data acquired from portable devices and sensors into useful information

© The Author(s), under exclusive license to Springer Nature Switzerland AG 2022
R. Mehra et al. (Eds.): ICCISC 2022, CCIS 1672, pp. 51–60, 2022.
https://doi.org/10.1007/978-3-031-22915-2_5

and to take meaningful steps taken in response to that facts [2]. It is crucial to consider the influence of IoT adoption in order to understand the problems and benefits of Internet of Things in Education, especially as IoT is still in its early stages in the education system. The Internet of Things provides numerous advantages, including: the development of intelligent interactive classes; the ability to customize dynamic models in which Students are active learners process; the encouragement of imagination; as well as real-time monitoring of students' cognitive processing. The COVID19 epidemic has put a strain on both research and the use of new technology in education. Higher interest in this study issue is indicated by an increase in the number of publications on the use of IoT in education, while contemporary educational practices are a factual evidence of such interest. Nevertheless, due to the fact that those possibilities are limitless within a cloud pack- age and educational process, this research focuses on providing the recent progress related to the cloud technology and IOT in education system along with its benefits and challenges.

1.1 Cloud Computing and Education

Cloud computing is a method of delivering a variety of services via virtual machines that are placed on top of a big pool of actual equipment in the cloud [3]. Services are stored in laboriously scalable information in visible form centers fashionable the cloud and accessed via the internet by some connected scheme. In the dispersed cloud environment, we have a lot of compute power and storage capacities. Some applications of cloud technologies in education are depicted in Table 1.

Table 1. Examples of the application of cloud technologies in education

Google Classroom [4]	Google Classroom is a cloud-primarily based totally gaining knowledge of control machine this is a part of the Google Apps for Education suite of products. Students can use Google Classroom on PCs, tablets, and cell-phones
Blackboard [5]	Education, mobility, communication, and trade software program, in addition to associated services, are furnished via way of means of Blackboard to customers together with instructional institutions, enterprises, and authorities agencies. In January 2014, round 17,000 faculties and businesses in a hundred nations had been the use of its software program and services
Knowledge Matters [6]	Knowledge Matters is a major virtualized online firm that teaches important business principles to college and high school students through interactive web, game-like business simulations
Coursera [7]	The most well-known educational site, in my opinion. Anyone can study a wide range of subjects on Coursera. There isn't a single student in the United States, Canada, Thailand, Russia, or Ukraine who isn't aware of Coursera's opportunity to gain valuable knowledge

(continued)

Table 1. (*continued*)

Microsoft Education Centre [8]	The Microsoft Education Centre turned into supposed to permit college students to retain studying irrespective of their circumstances. They make on-line studying viable and offer the best training to each and every student
Classflow [9]	Classflow is an interactive screen-based course delivery program that runs in the cloud. They offer customers unlimited access to lessons and learning tools without a subscription

1.2 IOT Enabled Education Environment

The Internet of Things is changing the way we live by transforming every product becoming an intelligent entity. All of this is correct in the teaching institution, where a veritable cycle of power is intelligently carried from Smart University, Smart Classroom, Smart Learning, Smart Learning and Smart Teaching to Smart Analysis (Table 2).

Table 2. Smart education

Smart Education	The purpose of smart education is to educate students with the skills and expertise they need to succeed in today's market. Smart education's success is dependent on sensing devices, an IoT infrastructure, communication linkages, and user apps. The IoT integration in the classroom institution would conclusion in higher educational quality since students will learn quickly and teachers will be prepared to carry forward their educational duties more efficiently [10]
Smart University	A smart university combines cutting-edge hardware and software, cutting-edge concepts, education techniques based on trendy, learning tactics, and smart teaching and smart classrooms equipped with cutting-edge technology [11]. A smart university has access to a diverse range of worldwide materials, an interactive teaching environment that can be examined inside the network, and learning that is flexible to data acquired. Many institutions have IoT devices such as temperature control devices, security cameras, electricity, heating systems, and building access devices
Smart Classroom	A smart classroom is a location where students can access educational activities utilizing electronic equipment such as internet-connected gadgets, digital screens and video projectors [12]. Beginning in 2012, a smart class is built on automated communication devices, mobile learning and mobile technologies, which use cameras, facial recognition algorithms, video projectors, sensors, and extra modules to keep track of many characteristics of the natural environments. When machines are linked to the Internet of Things, they form a smart class that allows access to knowledge from everywhere and at any time. A smart class offers numerous advantages, including greater information communication, flexibility, interactive learning, educational content exchange, and improved thinking capacities

(*continued*)

Table 2. (*continued*)

Smart Teaching	The manner in which information is transmitted via electronic devices can differ greatly from traditional teaching approaches. The material is always accessible, and Learning is adaptable, allowing you to stay up to date on the most recent advancements. The Internet of Things may provide access to the actual world, which might make teaching difficult because it must be adjusted and adapted to meet the needs of students with various impairments. Teaching methods must also be modified to accommodate students with disabilities
Smart Learning	Smart learning is a learning approach that makes use of electronic gadgets. According to [13], smart learning is a procedure that assists students in learning by focusing on the subject as well as the students themselves. This technology's intelligence, adaptability, and efficacy are dependent on the ICT infrastructure. The usage of Internet of things e-learning apps is critical for establishing a virtual classroom and a competitive learning process, both worldwide and locally. Because Students have access to every library or lab throughout the universe to collect data, conduct experiments, and send assignment or for self-evaluation and be assigned, the Internet of Things fosters online self-teaching
Smart Assessment	Smart assessment [14] goes beyond the traditional methods by adding other types of evaluation, such as interviews and focus groups. To make an accurate assessment, we must consider the effects of modern technology on how we work. The evaluation process then evolves as we engage inside an ever-expanding IoT ecosystem. To capture student behavior in online learning assessments, new learning systems must have the appropriate technologies. The Internet of Things instruments are available for use in assess the student's concentration, which is critical in assessing their education. It is feasible to design adaptive exams that are adjusted to the student's responses to questions and are presented in the student's preferred learning style. This type of examination would allow us to delve into the students' knowledge, how they understand and apply it, as well as their learning styles and skills. The usage of simulations during educational activities is an important component of smart assessment and can also be utilized as a learning approach

2 Literature Review

2.1 Cloud Computing in Education

In recent years, cloud computing implementations have attracted attention in several areas, including higher education in emerging markets. In this section we present a review of the adoption of cloud computing on education. Moodle was investigated [15] as a case of cellular cloud gaining knowledge of structures in better learning. Posted in [16] an overview on the use of mobile cloud computing (MCC) within the instructional field, which summarized the demanding conditions and troubles that MCC requires to gain knowledge of structures, as well as privacy, interoperability arise because of. The cognitive load on college students due to exceptional operating platforms, information integrity, community availability and community speed, and large learning materials and courses. Cloud computing (CC) in education was evaluated from the perspective of teaching staff and IT professionals in Saudi Arabia [17]. [19] The authors studied characteristics influencing adoption by collecting data from a mobile cloud learning environment from Blackboard users at the University of Leeds in the United Kingdom using a structured questionnaire. [20] The authors examined their country's potential to transition to remote mastering and reviewed structures that have been used in schooling and supported by government access, as well as modern online conversation structures. Those who are advanced with the help of using Microsoft Teams. [21] The authors noted China's revelations about the duration of the covid-19 lockdown with continued learning. Authors described technical support for instructors and knowing help for college students. [22] The authors examined the risks of using an automated machine and provided a web multi-element authentication test method. The authors [23] summarized the conditions of seeking to achieve the amazing distance of knowing and e-checking from the thoughts of professors and college students in Arab universities. Universities, schools and various educational institutions are important for the standard development of a country.

[24] Used the ambiguous AHP to take a look at the determinants of CC adoption in better Indian educational institutions. The maximum important factors decided to be relative profit, IT demand and security. [25] Using a SEM approach, the authors evaluated cloud computing-based education in Saudi Arabia and influenced characteristics such as reliability, social impact, information quality and ease of use. Tuan suggested that it would be more accurate to assess teacher research productivity using an integrated multi-criteria decision-making approach (MCDM). To do this, the researchers used the hybrid AHPTOPSIS technology. Due to the suspension of on-campus classes, a large jump in student ranks, monodemic content, and the content offered, and the material provided, e-mastering structures have grown at an exponential rate [26, 27]. The cloud era is now being used by many educational institutions, and it is very clear [28] that it has a shiny destiny.

In addition, due to the fact that there is a single database for all customers in the cloud, cyber security modifications can be analyzed and made quickly [29]. [30], as it was designed to allow customers to collaborate from anywhere at any time. It can reach out to more students outside the general study room and meet their needs. Due to better calls to keep education afloat, establishments are paying additional interest on a mix of cloud generation and e-learning. Almost all educational institutions saw it as a viable and suitable e-learning option. Nevertheless, the lack of study may also provide a theoretical framework on which to build a technology. On the other hand, the potential inherent in the cloud approach can also be highlighted as a major advantage in the development of an analytical framework and one-hit training techniques [31]. However, in the literature, common features of the cloud are associated with social participation and collaborative learning activities [32].

2.2 IOT in Education

The term "Internet of Things" (IoT) refers to state-of-the-art technology that connects all intelligent objects in a network without the need for human intervention. This is indeed a new study focus that would have recently discovered an important and compelling research base in a wide range of academic and industrial disciplines [33]. According to Walcott [34], many governments are implementing the latest digital defense strategies in the fight against COVID 19. During this time, digital technology and innovation gradually became the focus of mankind. The economic demands of COVID19 strongly drive the deployment and creation of new digital technologies at a particular pace and scale. Population surveillance, response assessment, incident detection and touch tracking is one of the digital tools used to facilitate the international public health impact of COVID 19, with a focus on public participation and data mobility. According to Islam [35], the integration of IoT with advanced technology could be a major step forward in efforts to combat new epidemics. The potential of the Internet of Things will have a significant impact on the ability of Western countries to achieve the SDGs (Sustainable Development Goals). In environments where Internet-ofThings-enabled devices and applications are used, it is essential to implement specified protocols, patient monitoring and primary identification procedures, to reduce the chances of spreading the coronavirus.

According to Jawed [36], the Internet of Things can send and receive both information and physical goods (IoT). Intelligent hospital equipment and concepts were controlled via wireless and wired Internet. Various medical diagnostics, instruments, advanced imaging equipment, artificial intelligence and sensors are essential for the implementation of IoT in the medical field. Intelligent technologies can collect and share data to carry out essential tasks in our daily lives. The application will pave the way for entertainment systems, automobiles, connected healthcare and smart cities. These advances have increased both the quality of life and the efficiency of industries and societies, both new and old. This technology is flourishing in health surveillance during the COVID 19 pandemic. According to Nasajpur et al. [37] Innovation has retained most of the information about COVID19 patients inside the data center to ensure adequate attention, and that could be more helpful. Internet of Things (IoT) combines all-digital, computing technologies and mechanicals to transmit data over the web without human intervention. In this dire scenario, many people die of late and incorrect medical information. The Internet of Things is taking over every day human activities and changing health problems. Sensors are used to quickly notify the system of health issues [38]. The successful operation of medical institutions requires proper equipment. During the COVID-19 pandemic, the use of the Internet of Things improves patient care. Smart medical devices are connected via smart connectors to deliver important medical data to doctors. These devices use the Internet of Things to successfully track real-time data, saving lives from a variety of health problems. The Internet of Things (IoT) has great potential to analyze and leverage impactful activities including after-services [36]. De Rauer and Radanlive [39, 40] focused on ethical IoT design updates and IoT design, but did not discuss the implications of the coupled and multiple risks of IoT system-themes. They concluded that before new ICT systems are incorporated, production facilities should be coupled with an ethical assessment of cyber threats. They enable governments, health experts, and medical organizations to build a framework to provide guidance in this article [41] as the introduction of IoT into the vaccination supply chain increases risk. [42] Applications of the Internet of Things include contact tracing devices, wearable health monitors, thermal cameras, temperature sensors and package tracking to help fight disease by providing critical data needed for the safe delivery of COVID19 vaccines. In this COVID situation, IoT has helped to make automated activities in warehouses and supply chains more resilient to encourage social distancing and secure remote access to industrial machines.

By studying the potential of IoT in the socio-economic development areas of Bangladesh, Parvez et al. [43] Created a conceptual framework model, and the model showed that Bangladesh needed to develop a set of policies for IoT deployment to implement a national strategy on the Internet of Things. Miyazi et al. [44] The IoT, introduced in Bangladesh, reveals technical challenges, financial challenges, security, privacy issues and device reliability, along with opportunities such as occupational safety, mHealth, traffic safety, service management and environmental monitoring. Sarkar et al. [45] Highlighting the future prospects and problems of some of the most promising IoT applications. As per the literature review on IoT applications in Bangladesh, no such in-depth work has been found on the current scenario of employing IoT in various industries during COVID-19. As a result, a conceptual model of the impact of Inter-Net of Things applications across multiple industries was created during the pandemic. During the pandemic, this study looks at the barriers and benefits of adopting IoT services across multiple sectors, and the findings will help organizations respond and adapt to IoT services more quickly, giving them a competitive advantage.

3 Discussion and Conclusion

In India, cloud computing adaptation in higher education is an under-studied area and the literature does not document systematic studies. We studied in this article how cloud computing can be used in educational contexts. Due to the COVID-19 pandemic which has prompted many schools, colleges and establishments to supply online training, it has become mandatory. According to the analysis' overview, using cloud services in E-learning is a good option since it allows teachers to take use of cloud adaptability, flexibility, and security to reflect the primary framework of E-learning education accessible from anywhere, at any time, and on any device. We can fully use the prospects presented by an efficient learning environment with specialized information that is easily adaptable to today's educational paradigm. Integrating an elearning system into the cloud has several advantages, including increased storage, computing, network connectivity and prioritize software and hardware cost savings. On the other hand, it offers a more diverse range of educational programs at a lower license cost. The replacement rate for student computers is lower due to the extended machine life. These savings add up to a reduction in IT personnel costs associated with computer lab maintenance and software updates. Today's e-learning services and systems are all about personalizing learning and learning for each user. As a result of this technology, students receive generic e-learning that is not tailored to their specific needs. In most modern systems, interaction between professors and students is essential for improving the quality of each student's learning experience. When evaluating the scale of a problem, there are many things to consider. In response to customer concerns about security and privacy, cloud service providers have made major investments in cloud infrastructure and platforms. Furthermore, country limits are necessary since some countries require data to be maintained within their borders, making data storage remotely or outside of the country illegal. As per current research, academics have a wealth of data at their disposal to aid in building cloud-based elearning frameworks and implementations. A quantitative assessment of the impact of switching to a cloud e-learning environment on several factors such as access speed, educational quality, and return will be conducted in the future. The adoption of IoT in universities may be influenced by education policy in terms of administrative support and change mindset. There is a need to examine the advantages and disadvantages of Internet of Things in depth. Information and communication technology (ICT), a society that places a high value on acquiring knowledge, and the current pandemic have all contributed to an increase in the amount of pressure on the education system to adopt ICT and make education more intelligent. There is also a need to explore machine learning algorithms [46–50] in cloud based analysis of education systems for tasks such as student monitoring, student lecture engagement, etc.

References

1. Dias, S.B., Hadjileontiadou, S.J., Diniz, J., Hadjileontiadis, L.J.: DeepLMS: a deep learning predictive model for supporting online learning in the Covid-19 era. Sci. Rep. **10**(1), 1–17 (2020)
2. Bagheri, M., Movahed, S.H.: The Effect of the Internet of Things (IoT) on Education Business Model, in Proc, pp. 435–441. SITIS, Naples, Italy (2016)
3. Gong, C., Liu, J., Zhang, Q., Chen, H., Gong, Z.: The characteristics of cloud computing. In: 2010 39th International Conference on Parallel Processing Workshops, pp. 275–279. IEEE (2010)
4. https://classroom.google.com/. Accessed 26 May 2022
5. https://www.blackboard.com/en-apac. Accessed 26 May 2022
6. https://knowledgematters.com/. Accessed 26 May 2022
7. https://www.coursera.org/. Accessed 26 May 2022
8. https://education.microsoft.com/en-us. Accessed 26 May 2022
9. https://classflow.com/. Accessed 26 May 2022
10. Mohanty, D.: Smart learning using IoT. Int. Res. J. Eng. Tech. 6(6), 1032– 1037 (2019)
11. Uskov, V.L., Bakken, J.P., Howlett, R.J., Jain, L.C. (eds.): SEEL 2017. SIST, vol. 70. Springer, Cham (2018). https://doi.org/10.1007/978-3-319-59454-5
12. Pai, S.S., et al.: IOT application in education. Int. J. Adv. Res. Ideas Innovations Technol. **2**(6), 20–24 (2017)
13. Gwak, D.: The meaning and predict of smart learning. In: Proceedings of the Smart Learning Korea (2010)
14. Aljohany, D.A., Mohamed, R., Saleh, M.: ASSA: adaptive E-learning smart students assessment model. Int. J. Adv. Comput. Sci. Appl. **9**(7), 128–136 (2018)
15. Wang, M., Chen, Y., Khan, M.J.: Mobile cloud learning for higher education: a case study of moodle in the cloud. Int. Rev. Res. Open Distrib. Learn. **15**(2), 254–267 (2014)
16. Sarode, N., Bakal, J.W.: A review on use of mobile cloud system in educational sector. In: 2020 6th International Conference on Advanced Computing and Communication Systems (ICACCS), pp. 715–720. IEEE (2020)
17. Almutairi, M.M.: A review of cloud computing in education in Saudi Arabia. Int. J. Inform. Technol. **12**(4), 1385–1391 (2020). https://doi.org/10.1007/s41870-020-00452-6
18. Kumar, V.: A review on deep learning based diagnosis of COVID-19 from X-ray and CT images. In: 2022 International Mobile and Embedded Technology Conference (MECON), pp. 547–552. IEEE (2022)
19. Sultana, J.: Determining the factors that affect the uses of mobile cloud learning (MCL) platform blackboard-a modification of the UTAUT model. Educ. Inform. Technol. **25**(1), 223–238 (2020). https://doi.org/10.1007/s10639-019-09969-1
20. Basilaia, G., Kvavadze, D.: Transition to online education in schools during a SARS-CoV-2 coronavirus (COVID-19) pandemic in Georgia. Pedagogical Research **5**, 4 (2020)

21. Huang, R.H., Liu, D.J., Tlili, A., Yang, J.F., Wang, H.H.: Handbook on Facilitating Flexible Learning During Educational Disruption: The Chinese Experience in Maintaining Undisrupted Learning in COVID-19 Outbreak, pp. 1–54. Smart Learning Institute of Beijing Normal University, Beijing (2020)

22. Mallik, S., Halder, S., Saha, P., Mukherjee, S.: Multi-factor authentication-based E-exam management system (EEMS). In: Bhattacharjee, D., Kole, D.K., Dey, N., Basu, S., Plewczynski, D. (eds.) Proceedings of International Conference on Frontiers in Computing and Systems. AISC, vol. 1255, pp. 711–720. Springer, Singapore (2021). https://doi.org/10.1007/978-981-15-7834-2_66

23. Bashitialshaaer, R., Alhendawi, M., Lassoued, Z.: Obstacle comparisons to achieving distance learning and applying electronic exams during COVID19 pandemic. Symmetry 13(1), 99 (2021)

24. Sharma, M., Gupta, R., Acharya, P.: Factors influencing cloud computing adoption forhigher educational institutes in India: a fuzzy AHP approach. Int. J. Inf. Technol. Manage. 19(2–3), 126–150 (2020)

25. Naveed, Q.N., Alam, M.M., Qahmash, A.I., Quadri, K.M.: Exploring the determinants of service quality of cloud E-learning system for active system usage. Appl. Sci. 11(9), 4176 (2021)

26. Khan, R.M.I., Radzuan, N., Farooqi, S., Shahbaz, M., Khan, M.: Learners' perceptions on whatsapp integration as a learning tool to develop EFL spoken vocabulary. Int. J. Lang. Educ. 5(2), 1–14 (2021)

27. Khan, R.M.I., Shahbaz, M., Kumar, T., Khan, I.: Investigating reading challenges faced by EFL learners at elementary level. Register J. 13(2), 277–292 (2020)

28. Khan, I., Ibrahim, A.H., Kassim, A., Khan, R.M.I.: Exploring the EFI learners' attitudes towards the integration of active reading software in learning reading comprehension at tertiary level. MIER J. Educ. Stud. Trends Pract., 248-266 (2020)

29. Bhardwaj, A., Goundar, S.: A framework to define the relationship between cyber security and cloud performance. Comput. Fraud & Secur. 2019(2), 12–19 (2019)

30. Kaisara, G., Bwalya, K.J.: Investigating the e-learning challenges faced by students during COVID-19 in Namibia. Int. J. High. Educ. 10(1), 308–318 (2021)

31. Park, J.H., Park, J.H.: Blockchain security in cloud computing: use cases, challenges, and solutions. Symmetry 9(8), 164 (2017)

32. Marinescu, D.C.: Cloud Computing: Theory and Practice. Morgan Kaufmann (2017)

33. Mohammed, T., Jean-Yves, C., Peter, B., Christophe, R.: Petrogenesis of the post-collisional Bled M'Dena volcanic ring complex in Reguibat Rise (western Eglab shield, Algeria). J. Afr. Earth Sci. 166, 102250 (2020)

34. Walcott, D.A.: How the fourth industrial revolution can help us beat COVID-19. In: World Economic Forum (2020). https://www.weforum.org/agenda/2020/05/how-the-fourth-industrialrevolution-can-help-us-handle-the-threat-of-covid-19

35. Islam, A., Anum, K., Dwidienawati, D., Wahab, S., Abdul, L.A.: Building a post COVID-19 configuration between Internet of Things (IoT) and sustainable development goals (SDGs) for developing countries. J. Arts Soc. Sci. 4(1), 45–58 (2020)

36. Javaid, M., Khan, I.H.: Internet of Things (IoT) enabled healthcare helps to take the challenges of COVID-19 pandemic. J. Oral Biol. Craniofac. Res. 11(2), 209–214 (2021)

37. Nasajpour, M., Pouriyeh, S., Parizi, R.M., Dorodchi, M., Valero, M., Arabnia, H.R.: Internet of Things for current COVID-19 and future pandemics: an exploratory study. J Healthcare Inf Res. 1, 40 (2020)

38. Fahrni, S., Jansen, C., John, M., Kasah, T., Körber, B., Mohr, N.: Coronavirus: Industrial IoT in Challenging Times. McKinsey & Company, New York (2020)

39. Radanliev, P., De Roure, D.: Alternative mental health therapies in prolonged lockdowns: narratives from Covid-19. Heal. Technol. **11**(5), 1101–1107 (2021). https://doi.org/10.1007/s12553-021-00581-3

40. Radanliev, P., De Roure, D.: Epistemological and bibliometric analysis of ethics and shared responsibility—health policy and IoT systems. Sustainability. **13**(15), 8355 (2021)

41. Radanliev, P., De Roure, D., Ani, U., Carvalho, G.: The ethics of shared Covid-19 risks: an epistemological framework for ethical health technology assessment of risk in vaccine supply chain infrastructures. Heal. Technol. **11**(5), 1083–1091 (2021). https://doi.org/10.1007/s12553-021-00565-3

42. Forum, W.E.: State of the Connected World (2020). http://www3.weforum.org/docs/WEF_The_State_of_the_Connected_World_2020.pdf

43. Parvez, N., Chowdhury, T.H., Urmi, S.S., Taher, K.A.: Prospects of Internet of Things for Bangladesh. In: 2021 International Conference on Information and Communication Technology for Sustainable Development (ICICT4SD), pp. 481–485 (2021)

44. Miazi, M.N.S., Erasmus, Z., Razzaque, M.A., Zennaro, M., Bagula, A.: Enabling the Internet of Things in developing countries: opportunities and challenges. In: 2016 5th International Conference on Informatics, Electronics and Vision (ICIEV), pp. 564–569. IEEE (2016)

45. Sarker, S., Roy, K., Afroz, F., Pathan, A.-S.: On the opportunities, applications, and challenges of internet of things. In: Khan, M.A., Quasim, M.T., Algarni, F., Alharthi, A. (eds.) Decentralised Internet of Things. SBD, vol. 71, pp. 231–254. Springer, Cham (2020). https://doi.org/10.1007/978-3-030-38677-1_11

46. Kumar, V., et al.: Hybrid spatiotemporal contrastive representation learning for content-based surgical video retrieval. Electronics **11**, 1353 (2022)

47. Kumar, V., Tripathi, V., Pant, B.: Learning unsupervised visual representations using 3d convolutional autoencoder with temporal contrastive modeling for video retrieval. Int. J. Math. Eng. Manag. Sci. **7**(2), 272–287 (2022)

48. Kumar, V., Tripathi, V., Pant, B.: Enhancing unsupervised video representation learning by temporal contrastive modelling using 2d CNN. In: 5th IAPR International Conference on Computer Vision & Image Processing (CVIP 2021)

49. Kumar, V., Tripathi, V., Pant, B.: Unsupervised learning of visual representations via rotation and future frame prediction for video retrieval. In: Singh, M., Tyagi, V., Gupta, P.K., Flusser, J., Ören, T., Sonawane, V.R. (eds.) ICACDS 2021. CCIS, vol. 1440, pp. 701–710. Springer, Cham (2021). https://doi.org/10.1007/978-3-030-81462-5_61

50. Kumar, V., Tripathi, V., Pant, B.: Exploring the strengths of neural codes for video retrieval. In: Tomar, A., Malik, H., Kumar, P., Iqbal, A. (eds.) Machine Learning, Advances in Computing, Renewable Energy and Communication. LNEE, vol. 768, pp. 519–531. Springer, Singapore (2022). https://doi.org/10.1007/978-981-16-2354-7_46

Smart Communication and Technology

An Effective Image Augmentation Approach for Maize Crop Disease Recognition and Classification

M. Nagaraju[1], Priyanka Chawla[2(✉)], and Rajeev Tiwari[3]

[1] School of Computer Science and Engineering, Lovely Professional University, Phagwara, Punjab, India
[2] Department of Computer Science & Engineering, National Institute of Technology Warangal, Hanamkonda, Telangana, India
priyankac@nitw.ac.in
[3] Systemic, School of Computer Science, University of Petroleum and Energy Studies, Dehradun, Uttarakhand, India

Abstract. Deep learning techniques have been applied to computer vision applications like image recognition and classification successfully. Especially, convolutional neural networks preserve the characteristics of an object in an image using kernels and performs recognition very efficiently. However, the performance of these networks depends on larger datasets which is a big challenge to the researchers in the agriculture field. Image augmentation can be a better solution that supports the neural network model to perform the classification task efficiently with more input images. In this paper, several image augmentation techniques were applied to generate varieties of new images from the original image. The paper proposes a new CNN-based model for the classification of six diseased and one healthy maize crop images. The proposed model will be trained for twice independently with 4652 original dataset images and 10640 augmented images dataset. Finally, the outcomes will be analyzed separately with respect to precise and loss functions. Before the implementation of augmentation approach, the proposed model has achieved 99.61% training and 77.44% classification accuracies and does not control overfitting. Moreover, after applying augmentation techniques, the model has obtained 95.96% of training accuracy and 93.61% of classification accuracy and controlled overfitting. Therefore, it has been proved that the image augmentation approach and the proposed convolutional neural network model contribute a better solution while classifying maize crop diseases with a higher level of accuracy.

Keywords: Computer vision · Convolutional neural networks · Deep learning · Image augmentations · Image classification · Image preprocessing techniques

1 Introduction

A practical approach to deal with less images in computer vision is typical. Augment the training images artificially can extract new images and may reduce overfitting [8].

© The Author(s), under exclusive license to Springer Nature Switzerland AG 2022
R. Mehra et al. (Eds.): ICCISC 2022, CCIS 1672, pp. 63–72, 2022.
https://doi.org/10.1007/978-3-031-22915-2_6

Imbalanced datasets can also be solved by applying augmentation techniques to transfer the original shape of the plant generating additional images [9]. Image augmentations gives a resultant dataset that is six times greater than the quantity of original set. The proposed model LeafGAN boosted the accuracy by 7.4% [2]. Model generalization can be improved by performing image preprocessing and augmentation. The experiments were conducted to evaluate the efficiency of the proposed model to classify DiaMOS plant dataset [3].

An advanced machine learning (ML) model is proposed to classify the major diseases in banana crop using ariel images. The results obtained by the trained models proposed that image augmentation have given positive outcomes on disease classification. The model has a control on training rate without any overfitting [4]. An image augmentation strategy has been followed to amplify the original images and tested the performance classification of apple. The results have shown that the proposed model achieved 6.3% higher recognition accuracy [3]. An enhanced classification model is proposed to increase the classification accuracy and address the overfitting problem. The model has achieved 24.4% higher overall classification accuracy using conventional image augmentations [1]. Synthetic image is the most usual method of data augmentation. The proposed model achieved 7% higher improved accuracy over the existing models [5]. A transfer learning concept has implemented by modifying VGG-16 to classify the images obtained from different mango farms. Image augmentation process is adopted and achieved 73% accuracy on the training dataset and 73% on the testing set. Data augmentation leads to 13.43% improvement on the testing data [7]. A conditional deep neural network is proposed for vigor rating of plants and investigated that after data augmentations the model has improved the classification accuracy and succeeded to obtain 23% increase in F1score. The proposed approach has resolved the problem of insufficient data size in plant diseases task [11–14, 12].

In this article, we have identified the need to expand all the seven datasets with data augmentation techniques. Image augmentation generates the new images that allows to balance all the disease classes with equal number of images. Firstly, an image of a diseased leaf with RGB representation is augmented into different variations for each transformation type. Seven types of image transformations like random rotation, horizontal shift, vertical shift, horizontal flip, vertical flip, random zooming, and random brightness are applied to an image of a diseased leaf. The outcome of these techniques generates a set of newly generated set of images that are used further to train a convolutional neural network (CNN). The novelty of the proposed work is to generate the new images dataset, design a CNN model, perform disease classification with original and augmented datasets.

The other sections are organized as: Sect. 2 discusses the approach followed to apply the image augmentation techniques. Section 3 describes the experimental results achieved from the image augmentation approach followed by the conclusion in Sect. 4.

2   Image Augmentation Approach

Image Augmentation or simple IA is an essential approach that replicates the given image with few transformations. The augmentation technique increases the diversity of images by changing each image in different ways like rotating, shifting, zooming, and flipping.

In this paper, a supervised learning named RGB Image Augmentation Approach (IAA) is followed to generate new images. The approach directs to improve the traditional techniques like augmentation by considering the requirement for new augmentation techniques. Figure 1 shows some original images and the images generated after applying the augmentations. The study employs the IAA as a preprocessing procedure to identify the converted images automatically. The newly generated images serve as the preprocessing procedure to feed the convolutional neural networks with the input images for training.

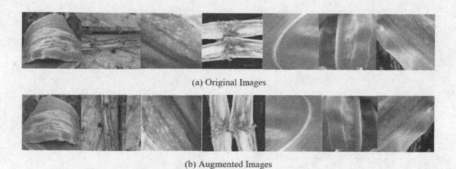

(a) Original Images

(b) Augmented Images

Fig. 1. Sample Images (a) original (b) augmented.

3 Experimental Results and Observations

A CNN model is developed to implement the IA approach and perform the image classification in this section.

3.1 RGB Image Augmentation

A new CNN model is developed with four convolution and max-pooling layers one and all continued with 1 flatten and 2 dense layers. Figure 2 shows the summary of the proposed model and the related hyperparameters are shown in Fig. 3.

3.2 CNN Evaluation

The classification performance of the proposed CNN model is evaluating by conducting the experiments with 4652 leaf images collected from Kaggle repository (Kaggle Dataset n.d.). These images belong to seven different classes of maize crop. The image dataset is split into two subsets as training set and testing set. IAA will be applied on the training images to generate new images with diffcrent variants. After applying IAA, the quantity of the training dataset is increased to 10640 images. The testing dataset is prepared with

```
Layer (type)                  Output Shape            Param #
=================================================================
conv2d_12 (Conv2D)            (None, 110, 110, 16)    448
_____
max_pooling2d_12 (MaxPooling  (None, 55, 55, 16)      0
_____
conv2d_13 (Conv2D)            (None, 53, 53, 32)      4640
_____
max_pooling2d_13 (MaxPooling  (None, 26, 26, 32)      0
_____
conv2d_14 (Conv2D)            (None, 24, 24, 64)      18496
_____
max_pooling2d_14 (MaxPooling  (None, 12, 12, 64)      0
_____
conv2d_15 (Conv2D)            (None, 10, 10, 128)     73856
_____
max_pooling2d_15 (MaxPooling  (None, 5, 5, 128)       0
_____
flatten_2 (Flatten)           (None, 3200)            0
_____
dense_6 (Dense)               (None, 128)             409728
_____
dense_7 (Dense)               (None, 7)               903
=================================================================
Total params: 508,071
Trainable params: 508,071
Non-trainable params: 0
```

Fig. 2. Proposed model summary

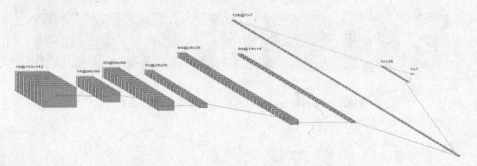

Fig. 3. The proposed 11-layer CNN model

2660 images that are randomly selected from the first dataset of 4652 images. The list of diseases and the number of images considered for each disease is depicted in Table 1. The model is evaluated with original and augmented datasets by training and testing individually. Later, the results obtained are used to validate and compare the actual predictions with respect to accuracy, loss and confusion matrix.

3.2.1   CNN Model Implementation

The present sequential model is designed with four convolution layers (Conv2D_1, 2, 3 and 4 layers) with kernel size 3×3 followed by four max-pooling layers with pool size 2 and 2 strides. The model has one fully connected layer, and two dense layers with 128 units for first and 7 units for the last layers. First, the proposed model is feed with original dataset (without augmentation) and performed the classification. Figure 4 shows the performance with training, testing accuracy and loss curves before implementing IAA. The accuracy and loss curves are plotted individually for better understanding and comparison of results.

Table 1. Details of training and testing datasets

Disease class	1	2	3	4	Total images
Anthracnose Leaf Blight - ALB	435	380	1520	380	2280
Anthracnose Stalk Rot – ASR	512	380	1520	380	2280
Eye Spot – ES	352	380	1520	380	2280
Gabriella Stalk Rot – GSR	452	380	1520	380	2280
Health – H	1320	380	1520	380	2280
Northern Corn Leaf Spot – NCLS	1170	380	1520	380	2280
Southern Rust - SR	411	380	1520	380	2280
Total	**4652**	**2660**	10640	**2660**	**13300**

1-Number of training images before IAA, 2-Number of testing image before IAA, 3-Number of training images after IAA, 4-Number of testing images after IAA.

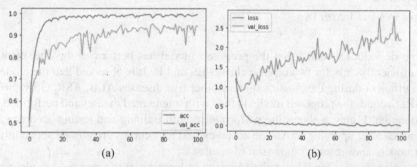

Fig. 4. Performance evaluation before applying the IAA technique

The plots in Fig. 4(a) shows the variation in learning of the proposed model using training and testing accuracies. The plots in Fig. 4(a) shows the variation in learning of the proposed model using training and testing losses. 'Acc' and 'val_acc' indicates the training and testing accuracy curves whereas 'loss' and 'val_loss' indicate the training and testing loss curves. The large gap between the accuracies and losses curves, a higher difference of 22.17% among the training and testing accuracies describe that the model is overfit to the training dataset and not performed the classification well on the testing set. Before applying IAA and after running the model using 100 epochs, the training accuracy of 99.61%, and the testing accuracy of 77.44% are obtained.

In addition to confusion metrics, the other performance metrics like precision, recall, and F1-score have also computed and the values are presented in Table 2. The confusion matrix of the proposed model shown in Fig. 5(a) and 5(b) revealed that the classification exhibited more than 95% accuracy in only two classes ES (95.7%) and H (97.8%). The precision metric values for ES and H disease classes are found as 93% and 91% respectively. The recall metric values for ES and H disease classes are found as 96% and 98% respectively. The F1-score metric value is reported as 96% for H disease class.

Table 2. Classification performance before and after applying IAA

Class #	1	2	1	2	1	2	Support
	Precision		Recall		F1-score		
0	0.61	0.89	0.71	0.95	0.65	0.92	380
1	0.87	0.97	0.89	0.90	0.88	0.93	380
2	0.78	0.94	0.96	0.94	0.86	0.94	380
3	0.93	0.88	0.98	1.00	0.96	0.93	380
4	0.91	0.95	0.71	0.94	0.80	0.95	380
5	0.59	0.95	0.58	0.87	0.59	0.91	380
6	0.77	0.98	0.59	0.95	0.67	0.97	380
		Accuracy			0.77	0.94	2660
Macro Avg	0.78	0.94	0.77	0.94	0.77	0.94	2660
Weighted Avg	0.78	0.94	0.59	0.94	0.67	0.94	2660

1-Before IAA and 1-After IAA.

The metric values revealed that the proposed model has performed the classification more efficiently only for two disease classes ES and H. It is observed that the model is not so efficient during the classification of other five diseases ALB, ASR, GSR, NCLS and SR. Second, the proposed model is feed with augmented dataset and performed the classification. Figure 6 shows the performance with training and testing accuracy and loss curves after applying IAA. The accuracy and loss curves are plotted separately or better understanding and comparison of results.

The plots in Fig. 6(a) shows the variation in learning of the proposed model using training and testing accuracies. The plots in Fig. 6(a) shows the variation in learning of the proposed model using training and testing losses. 'Acc' and 'val_acc' indicates the training and testing accuracy curves whereas 'loss' and 'val_loss' indicate the training and testing loss curves. The proposed model after training and testing with the images generated after applying IAA has obtained 95.96% training and 93.61% testing accuracies. A 2.35% difference among the accuracies between training and testing datasets shows that the model has performed well when compared the results obtained before applying IAA. The accuracy and loss curves describe that the present model is not overfit to the training images dataset and performed the classification well even on the testing dataset. The results shown in Fig. 6 explains that the proposed model is so efficient when it is trained with a greater number of input images. In this regard, image augmentation techniques have contributed a lot to increase the number of training images and achieve better classification performance.

In addition to confusion matrix, the performance metrics like precision, recall, and F1-score have also computed and the values are illustrated in Table 2. The confusion matrix of the proposed model depicted in Fig. 7(a) and 7(b) revealed that the classification exhibited 100% accuracy for H. The results exhibited more than 95% accuracy in only two classes ALB (95.2%) and SR (95%). It is observed that the classification exhibited

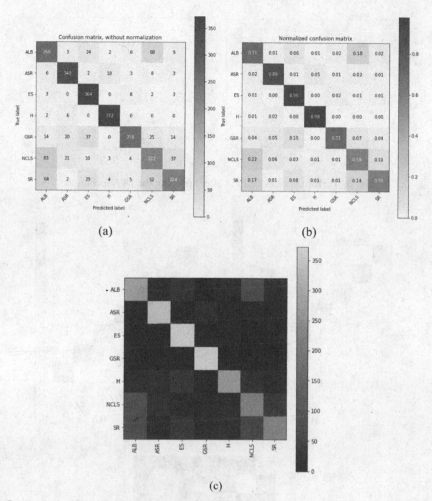

Fig. 5. Confusion Matrix before Implementing IAA Technique (a) without normalization (b) with normalization (c) color scale reflections

equal or more than 90% in two disease classes ES (93.6%), and GSR (94.2%). The classification exhibited equal or more than 95% accuracy in three classes ALB (95.2%), H (100%), and SR (95%). Precision metric values of ASR, ES, GSR, NCLS, and SR disease classes are found as 97%, 94%, 95%, 93% and 98% respectively. Recall metric values of ALB, ASR, ES, H, GSR, and SR disease classes are found as 95%, 90%, 94%, 100%, 94% and 95% respectively. The F1-score is reported 100% for H disease class. The results revealed that the proposed model has performed the classification of six disease classes ALB, ASR, ES, H, GSR, and SR more efficiently. It is observed that the model is not so efficient for classification of only one disease class NCLS. Figure 8 depicts the classification performance of the proposed model before and after applying IAA.

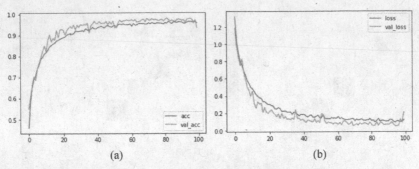

Fig. 6. Performance evaluation after applying the IAA technique

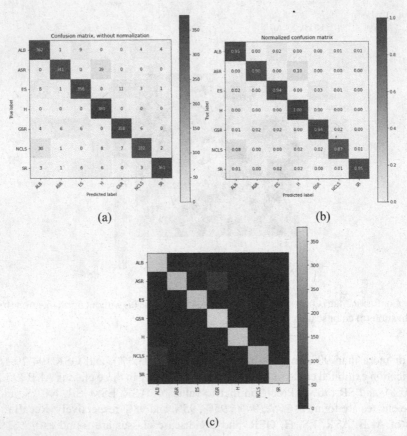

Fig. 7. Confusion Matrix after implementing IAA technique (a) without normalization (b) with normalization (c) color scale reflections

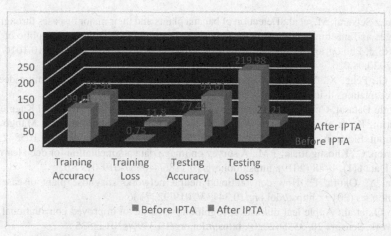

Fig. 8. Performance measure before/after IAA technique

4 Conclusion

An adoptive supervised learning approach IAA to perform image augmentations to generate the multiple images automatically in this paper. The enhanced dataset can be adaptive to train any CNN model. The present paper has proposed a new CNN-based model with 11 layers to perform the image classification of seven maize crop disease classes. Later, the model has trained and tested with different datasets. First, the model has trained with only 4652 images collected from Kaggle repository. Next, the same model has trained with 10640 augmented images. Finally, the accuracy and loss values have collected separately for two experiments and compared to identify the difference in classification performances. The first experimental results show that before applying augmentations, the proposed CNN model has obtained 99.61% training accuracy and testing accuracy of only 77.44%. The second experimental results show that after applying augmentation approach has obtained a training accuracy of 95.96% and testing accuracy of 93.61%. The observations have described that the proposed CNN model is so efficient while classifying the maize crop diseased and healthy images. CNN model is extremely effective when it comes to classifying the diseased images of maize crop. The findings drew attention to more advanced transformations for increasing the number of images in training set and assisting in the prevention of model overfitting.

References

1. Bi, L., Hu, G.: Improving image-based plant disease classification with generative adversarial network under limited training set. Front. Plant Sci. **11** (2020). https://doi.org/10.3389/fpls.2020.583438
2. Cap, Q.H., Uga, H., Kagiwada, S., Iyatomi, H.: LeafGAN: an effective data augmentation method for practical plant disease diagnosis (2020). http://arxiv.org/abs/2002.10100
3. Fenu, G., Malloci, F.M.: Using multioutput learning to diagnose plant disease and stress severity. Complexity (2021). https://doi.org/10.1155/2021/6663442

4. Gomez Selvaraj, M., et al.: Detection of banana plants and their major diseases through aerial images and machine learning methods: a case study in DR Congo and Republic of Benin. ISPRS J. Photogramm. Remote Sens. **169**, 110–124 (2020). https://doi.org/10.1016/j.isprsjprs.2020.08.025
5. Hu, G., Peng, X., Yang, Y., Hospedales, T., Verbeek, J.: Frankenstein: learning deep face representations using small data (2016). http://arxiv.org/abs/1603.06470
6. Kaggle Dataset: Corn or Maize Dataset Corn or Maize Leaf Disease Dataset | Kaggle (n.d.)
7. Kusrini, K., et al.: Data augmentation for automated pest classification in Mango farms. Comput. Electron. Agric. **179** (2020). https://doi.org/10.1016/j.compag.2020.105842 279
8. Shorten, C., Khoshgoftaar, T.M.: A survey on image data augmentation for deep learning. J. Big Data **6**(1), 1–48 (2019). https://doi.org/10.1186/s40537-019-0197-0
9. Toda, Y., Okura, F.: How convolutional neural networks diagnose plant disease. Plant Phenomics (2019). https://doi.org/10.34133/2019/9237136
10. Yan, Q., et al.: Apple leaf diseases recognition based on an improved convolutional neural network. Sensors **20**, 3535 (2020). https://doi.org/10.3390/s20123535
11. Zhu, F., He, M., Zheng, Z.: Data augmentation using improved cDCGAN for plant vigor rating. Comput. Electron. Agric. **175** (2020). https://doi.org/10.1016/j.compag.2020.105603
12. Mishra, A.M., Harnal, S., Gautam, V., Tiwari, R., Upadhyay, S.: Weed density estimation in soya bean crop using deep convolutional neural networks in smart agriculture. J. Plant Dis. Prot., 1–12 (2022)
13. Kaur, P., et al.: Recognition of leaf disease using hybrid convolutional neural network by applying feature reduction. Sensors **22**(2), 575 (2022)
14. Kaur, P., et al.: A hybrid convolutional neural network model for diagnosis of COVID-19 using chest X-ray images. Int. J. Environ. Res. Public Health **18**(22), 12191 (2021)

Implementation of Artificial Intelligence (AI) in Smart Manufacturing: A Status Review

Akash Sur Choudhury[1], Tamesh Halder[2], Arindam Basak[1(✉)], and Debashish Chakravarty[2]

[1] School of Electronics Engineering, KIIT, Bhubaneswar, Odisha, India
arindambasak2007@gmail.com

[2] Department of Mining Engineering, Indian Institute of Technology, Kharagpur, West Bengal, India

Abstract. In today's world, artificial intelligence (AI) is widely considered one of the highly innovative technologies. Usage of AI has been implemented nearly in all sectors such as manufacturing, R&D, education, smart cities, agriculture, etc. The new era of the Internet plus AI has resulted in the high-speed evolution of the central technologies, analyzed based on research regarding recent artificial intelligence (AI) applications in smart manufacturing. It is necessary to set up an industry that must be flexible with turbulent changes and adequately manage highly skilled employees and workers to design a more suitable working atmosphere for both men and technology. Google Scholar is widely used to explore several keywords and their combinations and search and examine the relevant articles, papers, journals, and study data for conducting this manuscript. The recent progress in intelligent manufacturing is discussed by observing the outlook of intelligent manufacturing technology and its applications. Lastly, the study talks about the scope of AI and how it is implemented in today's smart manufacturing sector of India, focusing on its present status, limitations, and suggestions for overcoming problems.

Keywords: Artificial intelligence · Smart manufacturing · Industry 4.0 · IIOT · CPS · Machine learning · Deep learning · RUL · ICT

1 Introduction

AI refers to technology having perceptive and psychological abilities. It has also authorized first-class coherent processes such as thinking, learning, perceiving, decision-making, problem-solving, data collection, segregation, and analysis to supplement human brainpower. In 1956, computer scientists Allen Newell, Marvin Minsky, John McCarthy, Arthur Samuel, and Herbert Simon developed artificial intelligence theory. Late in the 1990s and early in the twenty-first century, AI usage is rapidly transforming the globe, increasing the significance of analytics and enormous growth of computing ability [1]. Figure 1 tells us about the applications of AI/ML algorithms in different processes such as fault prediction, security, etc. In Fig. 2, various machine learning classifications and their characteristics are discussed. According to the training system and the input data type, there are three types of machine learning algorithm classifications:

© The Author(s), under exclusive license to Springer Nature Switzerland AG 2022
R. Mehra et al. (Eds.): ICCISC 2022, CCIS 1672, pp. 73–85, 2022.
https://doi.org/10.1007/978-3-031-22915-2_7

supervised learning, unsupervised learning, and reinforcement learning [2, 5].

Fig. 1. Applications of AI/ML algorithms [5].

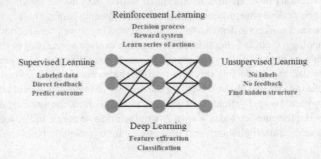

Fig. 2. Machine learning classifications and their significant characteristics [5].

Semi-supervised learning: this method has a small set of labeled information, and the remaining data is unlabelled hence the name semi-supervised.

Now smart manufacturing refers to the manufacturing technology aiming to provide the industrial setting for intelligent, real-time, autonomous, and interoperable production environments.

It integrates recent and innovative information and communication technologies (including 5G networks and Wifi), such as the Internet of Things (IoT), cloud computing (CC), and cyber-physical systems (CPS) powered by AI/ML decision-making technologies, and results in accurate fault detection and also real-time defective product recognition [3]. This paper describes the cycle of Industry 4.0, such as data acquisition, monitoring, connectivity, big data, smart assembling, control, and scheduling [47]. AI in intelligent manufacturing is utilized in various applications such as quality inspection, energy conservation, supply chain, and predictive maintenance [48]. The lifecycle of industry 4.0 in smart manufacturing is mentioned below in Fig. 3. While Fig. 4 describes the model of an intelligent manufacturing system and its applications [4].

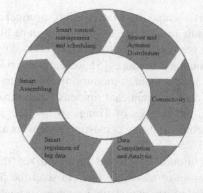

Fig. 3. Lifecycle of Industry 4.0 in smart manufacturing [47].

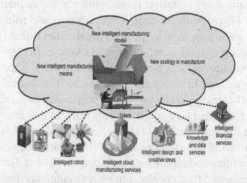

Fig. 4. Intelligent manufacturing model design [4].

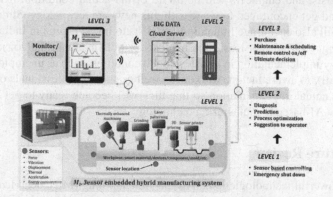

Fig. 5. Smart hybrid manufacturing system [2].

Autonomous sensing, learning, analysis, interconnection, cognition, decision-making, control, and information execution are included in the above figure, which integrates and optimizes the copious features of a manufacturing enterprise. AI-based

Smart manufacturing leads to enhanced worker safety, product quality, energy use, production efficiency, and fault predictions leading to a more high-yielding and secure workspace, thus engaging smart machines to carry out big tasks and assisting the human labor force getting rid of routine procedures [5]. Recently, the rise in usage of data-driven approaches has led to the achievement of monitoring and diagnosis by CPS observation and analysis that collect and communicate immense data through standardized interfaces, which gives rise to the Internet of Things [6]. Figure 5 shows an image of an intelligent hybrid manufacturing system consisting of sensors and new technology such as big data.

Machinery industries around the world have utilized the technology of smart machines and the automation of assembly lines to send the production data of these machines to a monitoring platform in real-time, such as inspection of ball-bearing malfunction, industrial data-driven monitoring, ball-bearing vibration data, remote wind turbine condition monitoring, vibration monitoring for smart maintenance and analysis of vibration time [7]. Significant cost reduction is made using predictive maintenance. This method can be proposed by prolonging the functional life of manufacturing machines and increasing overall equipment effectiveness [8]. In Industry 4.0 manufacturing, condition monitoring has been a valuable tool for improving safety, health, and equipment performance. In smart and sophisticated industrial equipment [9]. The knowledge-based intelligent supervisory system proposes a pattern recognition strategy and learning process to inspect rare quality events [10]. In this article, different types of ML and their applications in Industry 4.0 have been discussed. Also, how AI has taken place in Indian manufacturing, its scope, possibilities, and suggestions are discussed. This paper has been written to help future scientists to undergo further research regarding artificial intelligence and its algorithms in smart manufacturing. The article has also been reported to depict the Indian scenario in Industry 4.0. The Indian Government, Indian scientists, and engineers will be aware of the actual condition of Indian manufacturing and get encouraged to work with this new-age technology. Simultaneously, this article will also encourage Indian industrialists to invest capital in India's AI-based manufacturing. Last but not least, this manuscript tells us about the consequences of AI technology implementation in less developed countries, such as unemployment (due to lack of skill), to aware factory workers as well as skilled professionals of the reality regarding its actual implementation so that they will become ready to get accustomed with this new AI-based manufacturing technology.

2 Literature Review

AI and its powerful technologies, such as machine learning (ML), deep learning (DL), etc., are generally widespread in manufacturing. It has been evident that applying these technologies in real life requires enormous capital and efficient human resources capable of cooperative effort in surroundings [1]. The rapid advancement of machine learning has led to the massive revolution in the artificial intelligence field through which machines are allowed to learn, improve and optimize specific tasks without being programmed directly. Machine learning can be used widely in smart machining (consisting of CPSs) [2]. The Industrial Internet of Things (IIoT) provides real-time production data collecting with enhanced wireless connectivity, leading to Industry 4.0 powered by AI [5]. Remarkable progress has been made in recent years regarding database technologies, computer power, machine learning (ML), big data, and optimization methods to attain fault-free (defect-free) processes with the help of ISCS(Intelligent Supervisory Control Systems) [10]. Predictive model-based quality inspection is an innovative solution developed for industrial manufacturing applications using edge cloud computing technology, machine learning techniques, and IOT architecture. The quality inspection processes based on the predictive model are shown in Fig. 6 [11].

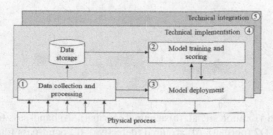

Fig. 6. Predictive model-based quality inspection framework arrangement [11].

Automation results in affordable cost, high reliability, and highly endurant quality inspection process in smart manufacturing industries. This helps to optimize high productivity, reliability, and repeatability. The automation process in manufacturing is run and regulated by a Programmable Logic Controller (PLC) [12]. Numerous applications of data science technologies or big data analytics in industries include process adjustment, monitoring, and optimization [13]. DL-based fault diagnosis of rotating machinery eradicates the drawbacks of traditional fault diagnosis methods [14]. Artificial neural networks (ANNs) have a long history of detecting equipment health conditions and RUL prediction in smart machines because of their effectiveness, adaptability, and many other factors [15]. If the engineers accurately implement inactive state detection in smart appliances in manufacturing, it will be beneficial in performing maintenance works, error reduction, and catastrophic failure detection [16]. The advancement of the IIoT has led to the rapid development and installation of sensors to monitor the machine condition and check whether the machine is operating and working correctly or not [17]. Incorrect readings and values of malfunctioning sensors can be estimated by accurately performing predictive analysis of big data, which can also be used in decision-making, including operation and maintenance planning [18]. Artificial intelligence, data mining, and other applications all use neural networks. A Deep Neural Network (DNN) is mainly proposed for non-linear high-dimensional regression problems, leading to the ambiguous process due to complexity [19]. Extreme learning methods are generally applied to eradicate the difficulties of a single hidden layer feedforward network and enhance generalization performance and learning capability [20]. One of the essential bearing types is the rolling element bearing. It is commonly used in the mechatronics field. The various bearing failures of rolling elements affect industrial equipment, such as productivity reduction, the rise of safety risks, and accuracy loss within this severe and harsh working environment. RUL (Remaining Useful Life) prediction is helpful in industrial manufacturing and production optimization [21]. The time-domain vibration signal features are extracted through fault diagnosis from the rotating machinery consisting of standard and flawed bearings. This can be possible with the help of ANN having input, hidden, and output layers [24]. Figure 7 shows various time-domain vibration signals.

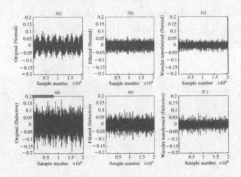

Fig. 7. Time-domain vibration signal: (a) acquired (normal), (b) band-pass filtered (normal), (c) wavelet transformed D2 (normal), (d) acquired (defective), (e) band-pass filtered (defective), (f) wavelet transformed D2 (normal) [24].

Machine learning techniques like neural networks help maintain and manage the considerable data complexities [23]. Cyber-Physical Production Systems (CPPS) and reducing this amount also helps to enhance machine efficiency, leading to more cost-effective output in industrial plants [22]. Data mining and ML (Machine Learning) algorithms can be executed to the data present in the SAP application to build classification models for predicting the reliability of industrial machines. [25]. Bearings are a crucial part of rotating machinery operation in most manufacturing systems. RUL and health analysis of bearings are performed to predict reliability and safety in manufacturing by increasingly providing powerful methods and processes that enable smart prognosis and bearing health management [26]. Defects present in rolling bearing may result in machine failure. But to avoid malfunctioning, early detection of faults is essential [27]. In comparison to other rotating machinery defects, rotor faults (mainly bearing and gear faults) have attracted more attention from the AI research community regarding the use of fault-specific traits in feature engineering [28]. Therefore, the vibration analysis technique predicts better reports in rolling bearing condition monitoring and fault diagnosis [46]. Oil and gas industry projects require colossal capital, including equipment acquisition and installation. The current drop in petroleum prices has limited spending, highlighting the necessity of proper maintenance management in the oil and gas business. Rotating mechanical equipment such as compressors, pumps, and induction motors are essential elements widely used in manufacturing procedures [28]. Image analysis powered by artificial intelligence enables accurate material characterization and measurement, displaying the quality of composite materials [30]. For the high-resolution images in the dataset, such as (the LCD panel cutting wheel degradation dataset), to enhance the computational efficiency, one will first extract the regions of interest from the raw image data, with 1400×80 pixels. After that, those regions are transformed into grey-scale images for further processing and then pretraining unsupervised data based on the dataset information [45]. Machine Learning and artificial intelligence will better identify failures, ensure quality, and improve preventative maintenance in real-world applications [31].

3 Methodology

We gathered, inspected, and clustered the data relevant to countless websites and different research papers as per the research requirements. The data has been collected from multiple websites together with the help of a brief introduction to AI technology and Industry 4.0. After that, the information was put compactly. Different AI and ML algorithms are used in smart manufacturing [1].

Table 1. Different models of prediction [11].

Model	Accuracy (%)	Stand ard deviation (%)	Recall (%)	Pre cision (%)	Training time (1000 rows) in ms	Scoring time (1000 rows) in ms
Naïve Bayes	83.5	±2.7	94.7	75.5	3	9
Decision Tree	88.2	±1.5	91.9	84.0	39	6
LR	71.9	±1.3	77.0	66.8	49	27
SVM	92.9	±1.3	96.4	89.3	300	360
GBT	92.6	±1.0	89.9	93.1	2	40

Methods such as CNN and ELM are applied in gearbox and motor-bearing datasets. The Continuous Wavelet Transform (CWT) is initially implemented to get pre-processed presentations of raw vibration signals. After that, the CNN algorithm is developed to extract high-level features, and ELM is further used to enhance the classification performance [32]. While ANN is used to classify the machine status into standard or faulty bearings, R-ELM is used to extract stator current vibration signals, detect bearing faults, and accurately achieve reliable classification, satisfying the need to see online bearing fault [33, 24]. The performance of different prediction models is shown in Table 1. Various signal processing techniques, such as STFT, WPT, FFT, etc., are proposed to overcome the challenges, such as removing background noise from vibration signals to extract the fault features with high resolution [34]. Mainly deep learning algorithms are used for regression of rotorcraft vibrational spectra [35]. Below at Table 2, it has been discussed about the input signal effect.

Generative Adversarial Networks (GAN) solve the current problems effectively encountered in defect examination of industrial datasets and identify unrevealed defects in future processing events, which led to its increased usage in Industrial Anomaly Detection [36]. In AI diagnostic techniques, spectral envelope analysis of the current remnant eliminates noise, manifesting the characteristic bearing faults [37]. Integration

Table 2. Effects of input signals on identifying machine conditions with five features (RMS, s2, g3,g4, g6) [24].

Case no	Input signals	Training success	Test success	Epochs
1	1	24/24 (100%)	13/16 (81.25%)	28
2	2	24/24 (100%)	14/16 (87.50%)	17
3	3	24/24 (100%)	12/16 (75.00%)	33
4	4	24/24 (100%)	15/16 (93.75%)	24
5	5	24/24 (100%)	15/16 (93.75%)	19
6	2,3	48/48 (100%)	32/32 (100%)	12
7	2, 3, 4	72/72 (100%)	48/48(100%)	22
8	1, 2, 3, 4	96/96 (100%)	63/64 (98.44%)	23
9	1, 2, 3, 4, 5	120/120 (100%)	79/80 (98.75%)	32

of RNN with LSTM can mitigate risk in rotating equipment predictive maintenance, leading to cost reduction in oil and gas operations [38]. GDAU Neural Network describes the tendency of rolling bearing degradation to have more vital short-term and long-term prediction ability, so it is more worthy for RUL prediction of bearings [21]. After undergoing extraction from the raw image data, the grey-scale images and pretraining unsupervised ML-based RUL prediction algorithms such as DCNN, DCNN-M, LSTM, NoAtt, and Nosupatt are used in the LCD panel cutting wheel degradation dataset containing images of multiple wheels having high-resolution. These RUL prediction methods provide a practical approach to prognosticative problems and partial observations [45]. Thus, recently there has been a rise in AI-based predictive maintenance and fault diagnosis in smart manufacturing, mechanical processes, and machinery.

4 Findings and Discussion

AI is a technology with perceptive and psychological abilities, having some high-yielding research relevant fields such as image processing, natural language processing, machine learning, etc., which is currently used in industry 4.0 manufacturing systems. Different manufacturing abilities such as Computer Numerical Control (CNC), automated guided vehicles (AGV), Direct Numerical Control (DNC), robotics, etc., are being used in smart manufacturing. Recently, the Internet of Things has taken manufacturing to another new level. The disadvantage is that, in many developing and underdeveloped countries such as India, there is a lack of resources to set up a basic structure; as most businesses operate in villages, there is a high cost of the smart infrastructure, skills, and training deficit among people in these technologies and a profitable proper investment put a barrier to implement this AI-based smart manufacturing technology. In less developed countries, unemployment is the central issue that led to numerous constraints in the absolute implementation of artificial intelligence. Other than that, according to experts AI and new age technologies only become a crisis for people who cannot adapt themselves, readjust according to the market's needs, or fail to become accustomed to new technology and skills, leading to joblessness. The probability of jobs in various fields due to artificial intelligence is shown in Fig. 8.

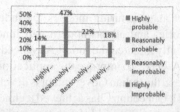

Fig. 8. The perceived probability of jobs due to Artificial Intelligence [45].

5 Research Limitation and Future Scope

Artificial intelligence and machine learning are extensively applied in today's world in different fields and purposes. Among them, smart manufacturing is one of the fields where the implementation of AI technology is at its peak. But, there are many ways to reap the benefits of artificial intelligence, such as smart maintenance, better product development, quality improvement, market adaptation, etc. Innovative care means maintaining manufacturing machines and systems more brilliantly, i.e., reducing the maintenance cost of appliances and types of equipment. As maintenance of equipment is one of the most significant expenses in manufacturing, it is necessary to implement smart maintenance such as predictive maintenance (powered by AI algorithms such as neural networks and machine learning), which will help save enormous amounts of money and enhance RUL of machinery. Through better product development, one can assess and examine the different parameters in production, such as available production resources, budget, and time, which can be implemented with the help of deep learning models and algorithms. To meet the highest standard and quality of products, machine learning, and machine vision can be used to identify, detect and eliminate faults in products and alert about the problems at the production line which may affect the overall production, leading toward production quality improvement. AI and ML techniques will help the smart manufacturing industries improve supply chains and strategic vision and make them interact with changes in the market by generating estimates relating to several factors like political situation, weather, consumer behavior, the status of the economy, etc. The utilization of AI, robots, and CPS will probably revolutionize mass production robots. CPS can perform any laborious tasks at high speed in smart factory units, eradicating human error and delivering superior levels of quality assurance. Unlike humans, AI and industrial automation can easily carry out tasks in hazardous places. Overall, AI-run smart machines can provide skilled workers, engineers, and scientists opportunities to focus on their complex and innovative functions in science, engineering, and technology rather than tedious and ordinary human tasks. But, the lack of necessary skills of workers regarding AI technology, especially in developing countries like India, may hinder the progress of AI in the Industry 4.0 manufacturing, which can only be solved by educating and equipping them with these AI-based technologies.

6   Indian Scenario

In India, Industry 4.0 smart manufacturing induces the industrial stalwarts to lay the groundwork for smart factories and adopt modern and innovative technologies. The Indian Government has recently initiated the Smart Advanced Manufacturing and Rapid Transformation Hub (SAMARTH). To improve the application of AI-based smart manufacturing in the current context, the Indian Government is developing a National Policy on Advanced Manufacturing [1]. Our country has achieved technological excellence by integrating Cyber-Physical Systems (CPS) and Information and Communication Technologies (ICT) into Advanced Manufacturing Technologies (AMTs). Increased automation in additive manufacturing, Advanced Manufacturing Systems, manufacturing robotics, advanced analytics, and Big Data are all worth mentioning in the design of smart manufacturing for Industry 4.0. They will help Indian MSMEs become more internationally competitive and contribute to global value creation [39]. Though adoption of artificial intelligence is less in India, there has been a remarkable transformation in all the Indian industrial sectors where companies are adopting, developing, and integrating AI technologies in their products and industrial processes, such as electronics, heavy electricals, automobiles, fintech, software/IT, agriculture, agrobased industries, etc. [40]. In terms of government funding, the Union Cabinet approved the launch of the National Mission regarding Interdisciplinary Cyber-Physical Systems (NM-ICPS) in 2019, which the Department of Science and Technology (DST) will execute with an unlimited budget of INR 3660 Cr (USD 494 Mn) for five years to make India a leader in Cyber-Physical Systems (which includes AI, ML, and IoT) (FY 2019–20 to 2023–24). The mission's goal is to build a strong and stable ecosystem for CPS technologies in India, which would help the country's Industry 4.0 manufacturing sector thrive [41]. SMEs have significant advantages in terms of innovation in general, but they face a variety of obstacles in India [42]. Though several countries have decided on their strategy for AI, India has not yet formulated its strategy in Industry 4.0 [43]. Another disadvantage is the lack of skilled workers in AI technology in our country; unemployment will rise in India. On one side cities will be equipped with all modern facilities and will be becoming smart and other side jobs will be killed due to transformation. Low and Middle skills level jobs will be shrunk, but high-skilled jobs where the critical decision will have to take will exist as machines cannot resemble human intelligence in case of making critical decisions. This transformation will add new development aspects to India's infrastructure and enhance the economic status in the coming years. However, few jobs in a few sectors will disappear because of transformation through AI in the next 5 to 10 years [44].

7   Conclusion

Although AI is still considered a nascent stage in Industry 4.0 manufacturing, one can still hopefully say that technological transformations are occurring. 5G technologies in communication can improve the overall efficiency and productivity, which has high network reliability and support IoT and CPS devices according to the industry requirements. Other advancements include lights-out manufacturing, which can create and regulate production with minimal human interaction, and smart and dynamic technology, which can be effective in areas with high production rates and low human error rates. Setting up an AI infrastructure platform may be costly due to advanced machines and equipment, but this reduces the labor required to finish the final product. But the advanced technology of AI-based applications in the Indian scenario will be extracted fully in the SME sector, which can be achieved 100% by providing incentives and encouragement to SMEs (because most of the people in India are employed in this sector). Similarly, the Indian educational system needs to be enhanced to enormously extract the potential benefits of these technologies.

References

1. Rizvi, A.T., Haleem, A., Bahl, S., Javaid, M.: Artificial intelligence (AI) and its applications in indian manufacturing: a review. In: Acharya, S.K., Mishra, D.P. (eds.) Current Advances in Mechanical Engineering. LNME, pp. 825–835. Springer, Singapore (2021). https://doi.org/10.1007/978-981-33-4795-3_76
2. Kim, D.-H., et al.: Smart machining process using machine learning: a review and perspective on machining industry. Int. J. Precis. Eng. Manuf. Green Technol. 5(4), 555–568 (2018). https://doi.org/10.1007/s40684-018-0057-y
3. Trakadas, P., et al.: An Artificial intelligence-based collaboration approach in industrial IoT manufacturing: key concepts, architectural extensions and potential applications. Sensors 20(19), 5480 (2020). https://doi.org/10.3390/s20195480
4. Li, B., Hou, B., Yu, W., Lu, X., Yang, C.: Applications of artificial intelligence in intelligent manufacturing: a review. Front. Inf. Technol. Electron. Eng. 18(1), 86–96 (2017). https://doi.org/10.1631/FITEE.1601885
5. Angelopoulos, A., et al.: Tackling faults in the industry 4.0 era—a survey of machine-learning solutions and key aspects. Sensors 20(1), 109 (2020). https://doi.org/10.3390/s20010109
6. Kumar, M., Aggarwal, A., Rawat, T.K.: Bat algorithm: application to adaptive infinite impulse response system identification. Arab. J. Sci. Eng. 41(9), 3587–3604 (2016)
7. Tsai, M.-F., Chu, Y.-C., Li, M.-H., Chen, L.-W.: Smart machinery monitoring system with reduced information transmission and fault prediction methods using industrial Internet of Things. Mathematics 9(1), 3 (2021). https://doi.org/10.3390/math9010003
8. McCulloch, W.S., Pitts, W.: A logical calculus of the ideas immanent in nervous activity. Bull. Math. Biophys. 5(4), 115–133 (1943). https://doi.org/10.1007/BF02478259
9. Hotait, H., Chiementin, X., Rasolofondraibe, L.: Intelligent online monitoring of rolling bearing: diagnosis and prognosis. Entropy 23(7), 791(2021)
10. Escobar, C.A., Morales-Menendez, R.: Machine learning techniques for quality control in high conformance manufacturing environment. Adv. Mech. Eng. 10(2), 1–16 (2018). https://doi.org/10.1177/1687814018755519
11. Pai, P.F., Hong, W.C.: Forecasting regional electricity load based on recurrent support vector machines with genetic algorithms. Electric Power Syst. Res. 74 (3), 417–425 (2005)
12. Ashwini, K., Rudraswamy, S.B.: Automated inspection system for automobile bearing seals. Mater. Today Proc. 46(10), 4709–5471 (2020). https://doi.org/10.1016/j.matpr.2020.10.301
13. Butte, S., Prashanth, A.R., Patil, S.: Machine learning based predictive maintenance strategy: a super learning approach with deep neural networks. In: 2018 IEEE Workshop on Microelectronics and Electron Devices (WMED), pp. 1–5 (2018)

14. Tang, S., Yuan, S., Zhu, Y.: Deep learning-based intelligent fault diagnosis methods toward rotating machinery. IEEE Access **8**, 9335–9346 (2020)
15. Tian, Z.: An artificial neural network method for remaining useful life prediction of equipment subject to condition monitoring. J. Intell. Manuf. **23**(1), 227–237 (2012). https://doi.org/10.1007/s10845-009-0356-9
16. Borith, T., Bakhit, S., Nasridinov, A., Yoo, K.-H.: Prediction of machine inactivation status using statistical feature extraction and machine learning. Appl. Sci. **10**(21), 7413 (2020). https://doi.org/10.3390/app10217413
17. Ertuğrul, Ö.F.: A novel approach for extracting ideal exemplars by clustering for massive time-ordered datasets. Turk. J. Electr. Eng. Comput. Sci. **25**(4), 2614–2634 (2017). https://doi.org/10.3906/elk-1602-341
18. Miorandi, D., Sicari, S., De Pellegrini, F.: Internet of things: vision, applications and research challenges. Ad Hoc Netw. **10**(7), 1497–1516 (2012). https://doi.org/10.1016/j.adhoc.2012.02.016
19. Beyerer, J., Usländer, T.: Industrial internet of things supporting factory automation. at-Automatisierungstechnik **64**(9), 697–698 (2016). https://doi.org/10.1515/auto-2016-0104
20. Ding, S., Zhao, H., Zhang, Y., Xu, X., Nie, R.: Extreme learning machine: algorithm, theory and applications. Artif. Intell. Rev. **44**(1), 103–115 (2013). https://doi.org/10.1007/s10462-013-9405-z
21. Qin, Y., Chen, D., Xiang, S., Zhu, C.: Gated dual attention unit neural networks for remaining useful life prediction of rolling bearings. IEEE Trans. Ind. Inf. **17**(9), 6438–6447 (2021). https://doi.org/10.1109/TII.2020.2999442
22. Kroll, B., Schaffranek, D., Schriegel, S., Niggemann, O.: System modeling based on machine learning for anomaly detection and predictive maintenance in industrial plants. In: Proceedings of the 2014 IEEE ETFA, pp. 1–7 (2014). https://doi.org/10.1109/ETFA.2014.7005202
23. Dubois, D., Prade, H.: Possibility theory is not fully compositional! A comment on a short note by H.J. Greenberg. Fuzzy Sets Syst. **95**(1), 131–134 (1998)
24. Krishnasamy, L., Khan, F., Haddara, M.: Development of a risk-based maintenance (RBM) strategy for a power-generating plant. J. Loss Prev. Process Ind. **18**(2), 69–81 (2005). https://doi.org/10.1016/j.jlp.2005.01.002
25. Shilaskar, S., Ghatol, A., Chatur, P.: Medical decision support system for extremely imbalanced datasets. Inf. Sci. **384**, 205–19 (2017). https://doi.org/10.1016/j.ins.2016.08.077
26. Rena, L., Suna, Y., Cuia, J., Zhang, L.: Bearing remaining useful life prediction based on deep autoencoder and deep neural networks. J. Manuf. Syst. **48**(C), 71–77 (2018). https://doi.org/10.1016/j.jmsy.2018.04.008
27. Gupta, P., Pradhan, M.K.: Fault detection analysis in rolling element bearing: a review. Mater. Today Proc. **4**(2), 2085–2094 (2017)
28. Nath, A.G., Udmale, S.S., Singh, S.K.: Role of artificial intelligence in rotor fault diagnosis: a comprehensive review. Artif. Intell. Rev. **54**(4), 2609–2668 (2020). https://doi.org/10.1007/s10462-020-09910-w
29. Golub, T.R., et al.: Molecular classification of cancer: class discovery and class prediction by gene expression monitoring. Science **286**(5439), 531–7 (1999). https://doi.org/10.1126/science.286.5439.531
30. Aggour, K.S., et al.: Artificial intelligence/machine learning in manufacturing and inspection: a GE perspective. MRS Bull. **44**(7), 545–558 (2019). https://doi.org/10.1557/mrs.2019.157
31. Mohapatra, P., Chakravarty, S., Dash, P.K.: Microarray medical data classification using kernel ridge regression and modified cat swarm optimization based gene selection system. Swarm Evolut. Comput. **28**, 144–60 (2016). https://doi.org/10.1016/j.swevo.2016.02.002
32. Chen, Z., Gryllias, K., Li, W.: Mechanical fault diagnosis using convolutional neural networks and extreme learning machine. Mech. Syst. Signal Process. **133**(1), 106272 (2019). https://doi.org/10.1016/j.ymssp.2019.106272

33. Zhang, H.-G., Zhang, S., Yin, Y.-X.: A novel improved ELM algorithm for a real industrial application. Math. Probl. Eng. **2**, 1–7 (2014). https://doi.org/10.1155/2014/824765
34. García-Nieto, J., Alba, E.: Parallel multi-swarm optimizer for gene selection in DNA microarrays. Appl. Intell. **37**(2), 255–266 (2012). https://doi.org/10.1007/s10489-011-0325-9
35. Martinez, D., Brewer, W., Behm, G., Strelzoff, A., Wilson, A., Wade, D.: Deep learning evolutionary optimization for regression of rotorcraft vibrational spectra. In: 2018 IEEE/ACM Machine Learning in HPC Environments (MLHPC), pp. 57–66 (2018). https://doi.org/10.1109/MLHPC.2018.8638645
36. Wang, A., An, N., Chen, G., Yang, J., Li, L., et al.: Incremental wrapper based gene selection with Markov blanket. In: 2014 IEEE International Conference on Bioinformatics and Biomedicine (BIBM), pp. 74–79. IEEE (2014). https://doi.org/10.1109/BIBM.2014.6999251
37. Bolón-Canedo, V., Sánchez-Maroño, N., Alonso-Betanzos, A.: Distributed feature selection: an application to microarray data classification. Appl. Soft Comput. **30**, 136–150 (2015). https://doi.org/10.1016/j.asoc.2015.01.035
38. Chazhoor, A., Mounika, Y., Vergin Raja Sarobin, M., Sanjana, M.V., Yasashvini, R.: Predictive maintenance using machine learning based classification models. IOP Conf. Ser. Mater. Sci. Eng. **954**(1) (2020). https://doi.org/10.1088/1757899X/954/1/012001
39. Sankararaju, M., Dharmar, S.: Design of low power CMOS LC VCO for direct conversion transceiver. Turk. J. Electr. Eng. Comput. Sci. **24**(4), 3263–3273 (2016)
40. Hossain, M., Muhammad, G., Guizani, N.: Explainable AI and mass surveillance system-based healthcare framework to combat COVID-19 like pandemics. IEEE Network **34**(4), 126–132 (2020). https://doi.org/10.1109/MNET.011.2000458
41. Acar, E., Yilmaz, I.: COVID-19 detection on IBM quantum computer with classical-quantum transfer learning. Turk. J. Electr. Eng. Comput. Sci. **29**(1), 46–61 (2021). https://doi.org/10.3906/elk-2006-94
42. Krishnaswamy, K.N., Bala Subrahmanya, M.H., Mathirajan, M.: Technological innovation induced growth of engineering industry SMEs: case studies in Bangalore. Asian J. Innov. Policy **4**(2), 217–41(2015). https://doi.org/10.7545/AJIP.2015.4.2.217
43. Conti, M, Dehghantanha, A., Franke, K., Watson, S.: Internet of things security and forensics: challenges and opportunities. Future Gener. Comput. Syst. **78**(2), 544–546 (2018). https://doi.org/10.1016/j.future.2017.07.060
44. Mendoza, C.V., Kleinschmidt, J.H.: Mitigating on-off attacks in the Internet of Things using a distributed trust management scheme. Int. J. Distrib. Sens. Netw. **11**(11), 859731 (2015)
45. Chen, R., Guo, J., Bao, F.: Trust management for SOA-based IoT and its application to service composition. IEEE Trans. Serv. Comput. **9**(3), 482–95 (2014)
46. Abderrahim, O.B., Elhedhili, M.H., Saidane, L.: DTMS-IoT: a Dirichlet-based trust management system mitigating OnOff attacks and dishonest recommendations for the Internet of Things. In: IEEE/ACS 13th International Conference of Computer Systems and Applications (AICCSA), Agadir, Morocco, pp. 1–8 (2016)
47. Zheng, P., et al.: Smart manufacturing systems for Industry 4.0: conceptual framework, scenarios, and future perspectives. Front. Mech. Eng. **13**(?), 137–150 (2018). https://doi.org/10.1007/s11465-018-0499-5
48. Ding, H., Gao, R.X., Isaksson, A.J., Landers, R.G., Parisini, T., Yuan, Y.: State of AIBased monitoring in smart manufacturing and introduction to focused section. IEEE/ASME Trans. Mechatron. **25**(5), 2143–2154 (2020). https://doi.org/10.1109/TMECH.2020.3022983

Emerging Computing Computational
Intelligence

Flight Fare Prediction Using Machine Learning

K. P. Arjun[1][✉] [iD], Tushar Rawat[2] [iD], Rohan Singh[2] [iD], and N. M. Sreenarayanan[1] [iD]

[1] Department of Computer Science and Engineering, GITAM University, Bengaluru, Karnataka, India
arjunkppc@gmail.com, sree.narayanan1@gmail.com

[2] School of Computer Science and Engineering, Galgotias University, Greater Noida, Uttar Pradesh, India
tusharrawat517@gmail.com, rohansingh7217@gmail.com

Abstract. The price of airline tickets can fluctuate gradually and generally with the same aircraft, independent of, in the seats that are closest together inside the same cabinet. Customers have the expectation that they will pay decreased expenses, whereas airlines work to maintain or even increase their overall earnings while also working to improve their profitability. To maximise their payload, airlines employ a variety of mathematical methods, such as guessing and suitable classification, among others. Models that estimate the best open door buy and models that anticipate the cost of a basic ticket are the two sorts of client-side models that various industry professionals recommend in order to save clients money. Both of these models fall under the category of client-side predictive models. According to our research, models on both sides depend on the restricted performance of several components, such as actual ticket price data, the date the ticket was purchased, and the date the passenger exited the venue. Many individuals take flights on a regular basis, and as a result, they are familiar with the times of year that provide the best deals on airline tickets. Despite this, there are a great number of individuals who have recently purchased tickets but wind up falling prey to the snares made by organisations, as a result of which they wind up spending more money than they should have.

Keywords: Airline price · Machine learning · Flutter · Flask · Random Forest · Flight ticket

1 Introduction

Calculations of forecasts are essential to the process of matching customers with the appropriate products and typically involve the use of real customer data. A related condition does not strictly anticipate the future item but rather suggests an item that does not occur in the actual information but that the customer could appreciate. In most cases, the focus of these proposal methods is positioned appropriately at the appropriate point in a sequence [1].

Despite this, there are situations in which it is necessary to predict as well as maybe suggest. A good illustration of this is the process of booking flights, in which the objective

© The Author(s), under exclusive license to Springer Nature Switzerland AG 2022
R. Mehra et al. (Eds.): ICCISC 2022, CCIS 1672, pp. 89–99, 2022.
https://doi.org/10.1007/978-3-031-22915-2_8

examples for the guaranteed customer might either be constant or change depending on a huge number of complex elements [2].

This challenging combat booking area is the focal point of this study, with a specific interest in measuring client ways of behaving for this mixed forecast proposal environment. Specifically, this exploration has a specific interest in gauging client ways of behaving. Researching the efficacy of algorithmic ways in suggesting the following objective reserving for a carrier client is the purpose of our examination. The vast majority of the previous work in both the expectation and suggestion sectors has been developed and evaluated solely on verifiable datasets. This is true of both regions. A limited number of earlier examinations have conducted research with actual customers to evaluate the generated models. In the course of this investigation, we conduct evaluations using both genuine information and actual customers [3].

The purpose of this effort is to promote the development of an application that will use the AI model to predict the cost of flight for a variety of airlines. The customer will receive the features that were anticipated, and using it as a reference, the customer may choose to purchase his tickets in the same manner. As a result of the same problem, airlines are attempting to keep a tighter rein on the prices of their tickets in order to boost their earnings [4]. Numerous individuals have made flying their primary mode of transportation, and as a result, they are constantly on the lookout for ways to cut costs when they make their reservations. However, there are a lot of people who are not used to purchasing tickets, and as a result, they frequently find themselves falling into the wrong trap set by organisations, which results in them paying more money than they should have. The proposed structure has the potential to assist clients save a significant amount of rupees by displaying booking information to them via the most advantageous open door [5]. We have constructed a model out of wood, however it is not appropriate for use in estimating the cost of aircraft due to the many different aspects that play a role in determining the cost of aircraft [6].

To estimate future trip costs, our team came up with the Random Forest Regression Algorithm as a result of the fact that it employs both regression and classification in its prediction-making process, resulting in a more precise outcome. The research that we carried out lends credence to this notion [7].

The cost of airline tickets can be hard to see, today we can see the price, see the cost of the same flight tomorrow will be another matter. We may have often heard travelers say that the cost of airline tickets is unpredictable [8]. Air travel has become an important means of transportation travel a significant distance. To maximize profits, airlines use an integrated pricing system called "yield the board" to calculate the cost of each trip. Competition, etc. The ultimate goal of earning extra profit on each aircraft. Since travelers are generally willing to admit that air travel costs are increasing when the purchase date is closer to the departure date, they usually purchase airline tickets from a city farther away from the departure date as expected [9]. However, buying this way is not right. It is like failing and in the process the passenger will be spending a lot of money.

After modeling the guessing system, it was important to make a visual interface that is easy to use and can be used on any device running on any operating system. AI is a mathematical investigation that will work best through experience [10]. Officially he works at work, based on performance, due to involvement. It is a topic under Artificial Intelligence. While AI controls the in-depth functions performed by a non-human professional, ML controls selective knowledge-based choices. AI is a very large field in software engineering. AI can be redirected, or on the other hand can be redirected. Problems in ML included. Compilation: if a few details are given, we need to plan a specific way to put it together. Repetition: given a small amount of information, can we expect the results to be respected? The information used in ML can be of three types: Categorical Nominal, Categorical Ordinal, and Continuous. We look forward to working with duplicate models that we suspect can provide us with more accurate results. Filtered models to work with [11].

In fact, it is undoubtedly a challenge for travelers to foresee when the best opportunity to buy war tickets is for the following reasons:

- Incomplete Information: Travelers can access part of the network carrier data. Truth be told, they do not have access to important information, such as the number of extra tickets and understanding between network company organizations [12].
- Different Information: Data that can be obtained by sailors is categorized. For example, it is undoubtedly a challenge for the average inspector to find a relationship between flight costs and flight costs, such as travel expenses, departure time, and so on.
- Unusual Changes: Although inspectors cannot collect a guaranteed flight amount, the cost change is not smooth. In fact, not all reports are predictable. So, travelers can only anticipate future flight costs with great effort in terms of recorded prices.

2   Literature Review

A dataset consisting of 1814 information trips on Aegean Airlines was gathered and used to prepare an artificial intelligence model for the research work. This procedure was used for the research work that was proposed by K. Tziridis T [13] on air fare cost expectation using machine learning procedure. To demonstrate how the identification of highlights can affect the accuracy of a model, a varied number of elements was used to prepare each model.

The next piece of research to be provided is a concentration on suggestion that William Forests, an expert, should work on improving buy timing for customers. In order to construct a model, an incomplete least square relapse technique is applied.

A study on aeroplane passage anticipation using AI calculation uses a small dataset consisting of travels between Delhi and Bombay, as stated by the author Supriya Rajankar [14]. The calculations K-closest neighbours (KNN), straight relapse, and support vector machine (SVM), among others, are applied.

Research carried out by Santos [15] investigates the cost of flying from Madrid to London, Frankfurt, New York, and Paris over the course of a few short months. The number of days that are considered to be adequate before booking an airline ticket is provided by the model. Tianyi Wang [16] developed a framework in which two information bases are integrated along with information regarding macroeconomics and artificial intelligence calculations, such as support vector machine.

The aforementioned algorithms each have their own drawbacks, such as the fact that there is not enough data in the system to make an accurate prediction. The accuracy of the system shifts whenever the algorithm is altered, which can make things a little bit confused, despite the fact that the accuracy shifts significantly only when essential elements are disabled. These studies are now considered to be obsolete as a result of the proliferation of new airlines, significant shifts in the cost of oil, and rising prices for a variety of other goods and services [17–20].

3 Proposed Methodology

In order to predict the price of a plane it was necessary to consider all possible parameters and how it effects the price of the aircraft in order to improve the Random Forest machine model which provides almost the most accurate result based on the data provided. Table 1 represents the columns name and its description.

Table 1. Parameters for price prediction.

Name	Description
Origin	The place where flight will star from
Destination	Place where the flight has to reach
Departure date	The departure date of the flight
Arrival date	The arrival date of the flight
Departure time	The departure time of the flight "HH:MM"
Arrival time	The arrival time of the flight "HH:MM"
Airline company	The airline company whose flight we are using
Duration	Total time taken by the flight to complete the journey
Stops	Number of stops between origin and destination

To make a for "Airfare Prediction", model in light of past carrier ticket deals dataset for further developing deals in Indian Domestic Airline. Our fundamental thought process is to furnish the client with a forecast framework from which it can take an ideal choice of expanding or diminishing the Airfare so the flight doesn't go unfilled or no cash is lost because of unexpected expansion in unrefined petroleum [8].

a) To perform information investigation on client's ticket booking information for a short measure of time.

b) To refine the information for example Eliminating copy records, vagueness and so forth.
c) To perform Feature designing to separate significant component from dataset for expectation.
d) To Brainstorm the Features for example to choose how to utilize those elements
e) To make highlights for example to get new highlights from those helpful elements.

The proposed framework is made out of four stages [13]:

1. Dataset Selection
2. Data Cleaning
3. Feature Extraction
4. Machine Learning Model Selection

3.1 Information Input

Input data is given to the system in the form of a.csv file. The dataset that was chosen from Kaggle serves as both the training dataset and the testing dataset. The data only pertain to flights within the country. In total, our dataset is comprised of 11 columns. [https://www.kaggle.com/datasets/shubhambathwal/flight-price-prediction]. Figure 1 shows the columns header listing.

```
        train_data.info() #object data types it is a string
[6]

...   <class 'pandas.core.frame.DataFrame'>
      RangeIndex: 10683 entries, 0 to 10682
      Data columns (total 11 columns):
       #   Column           Non-Null Count  Dtype
      ---  ------           --------------  -----
       0   Airline          10683 non-null  object
       1   Date_of_Journey  10683 non-null  object
       2   Source           10683 non-null  object
       3   Destination      10683 non-null  object
       4   Route            10682 non-null  object
       5   Dep_Time         10683 non-null  object
       6   Arrival_Time     10683 non-null  object
       7   Duration         10683 non-null  object
       8   Total_Stops      10682 non-null  object
       9   Additional_Info  10683 non-null  object
       10  Price            10683 non-null  int64
      dtypes: int64(1), object(10)
      memory usage: 918.2+ KB
```

Fig. 1. Columns in training dataset

3.2 Data Cleaning

The process of cleaning data involves removing any instances of null values from the dataset and replacing them with more appropriate values. These values are typically the mean, median, or mode of the other data in the column. The presence of null values in the dataset may have an impact on the accuracy of the model. The data cleaning steps shows in Fig. 2.

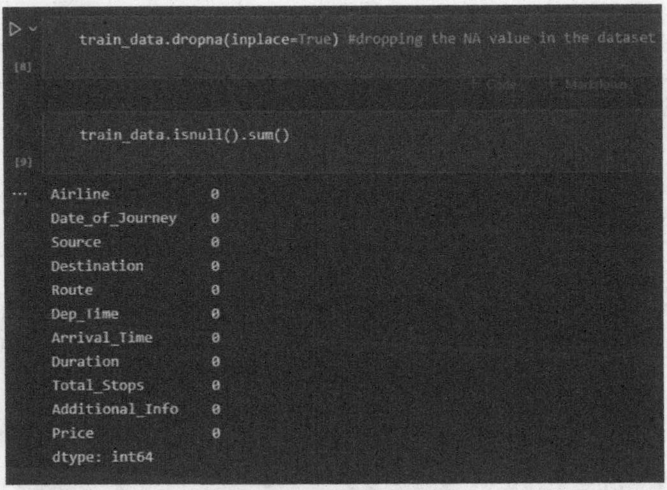

```
▷ ˅      train_data.dropna(inplace=True) #dropping the NA value in the dataset
  [8]


         train_data.isnull().sum()
  [9]

···   Airline              0
      Date_of_Journey      0
      Source               0
      Destination          0
      Route                0
      Dep_Time             0
      Arrival_Time         0
      Duration             0
      Total_Stops          0
      Additional_Info      0
      Price                0
      dtype: int64
```

Fig. 2. Cleaning of data

3.3 Feature Extraction

In this phase we try to extract new features from the dataset which will help to train model more accurate and prediction becomes easy and convenient shows in Fig. 3. New Features is added to the dataset which becomes the discriminating factor of price of flight and the reason of their variation. Figure 4 shows the correlation between the different feature in the dataset.

Features that can be considered as deciding factor of flight fare are.

- Feature 1: date and time of time
- Feature 2: date and time of departure
- Feature 3: How the early the ticket is booked
- Feature 4: Type of passenger (Adult/Child)
- Feature 4: Class of the flight booked (Economy/Business)
- Feature 5: Departure Location
- Feature 6: Destination Location

```
#since we have converted Date_of_Journey
train_data.drop(["Date_of_Journey"],axis=1,inplace=True)
[13]

#depature time is when a plane leaves the gate.
#extracting Hours
train_data["Dep_hour"]=pd.to_datetime(train_data["Dep_Time"]).dt.hour
#Extracting Minuminute
train_data["Dep_min"]=pd.to_datetime(train_data["Dep_Time"]).dt.minute
#Now we can drop Dep_Time as it is of no use
train_data.drop(["Dep_Time"],axis=1,inplace=True)
#Arrival time is when the plane pulls up to the gate
#extracting Hours
train_data["Arrival_hour"]=pd.to_datetime(train_data.Arrival_Time).dt.hour
#extracting Minutes
train_data["Arrival_min"]=pd.to_datetime(train_data.Arrival_Time).dt.minute
[14]
```

Fig. 3. Feature extraction in model.

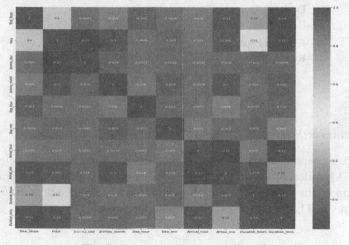

Fig. 4. Correlation between attributes

3.4 Machine Learning Model Selection

There are bunch of Machine Learning algorithm to choose from each having their own pros and cons. Linear regression being easy to train and simple to test but with less accuracy we decide not to move forward with it. Decision trees are essentially of two kinds of arrangement and regression tree where arrangement is utilized for unmitigated values and regression is utilized for persistent qualities. Decision tree picks autonomous variable from dataset as choice hubs for independent direction.

Random forest fundamentally utilizes gathering of decision trees as gathering of models. Random amount of information is passed to choice trees and every decision tree predicts values as indicated by the dataset given to it. From the expectations went with by the decision trees the typical worth of the anticipated qualities whenever considered as the result of the arbitrary woods model. Since it uses both regression and classification we find it to be the best fit for our system.

4 Result and Discussions

In proposed work, developed various algorithms such as Linear Regression, Decision Tree Decision, Random Forest Depression and compared the accuracy of the results based on our set of experimental data. Based on various levels of accuracy we find that the Random Forest Regression provides the highest accuracy at 81% shows in Table 2. So we selected Random Forest Resolve and built user interface based on it.

Table 2. Accuracy of different algorithms

Algorithms	Accuracy
Linear Regression	0.61
Decision Tree Regression	0.64
Random Forest Regression	0.85

4.1 Performance Metrics

Performance measurements are validated models that will be used to determine the accuracy of AI models suitable for various calculations. The sklearn.metrics module will be used to apply the deficiencies in each model using backslide scales. The following measurements will be used to assess the bumble level of each model.

4.1.1 MAE (Mean Absolute Error)

A small component of mathematical accuracy is called the Mean Absolute Error (MAE) as Eq. 1. Mean Absolute Error is basically, as the name suggests, a description of obvious errors. Direct error is the actual value of the difference between the expected value and the actual value. It Means Perfect Error It means measuring accuracy of a fixed object.

$$MAE = \tfrac{1}{n} \left[\sum |x - \hat{x}| \right] \tag{1}$$

n = the number of errors,
Σ = summation symbol (which means "add them all up"),
$|x - \hat{x}|$ = the absolute errors.
Lesser the value of MAE the better the performance of your model.

4.1.2   MSE (Mean Square Error)

Mean Square Error squares the distinction of real and anticipated result esteems prior to adding them all rather than utilizing the outright worth shows in Eq. 2.

$$MSE = \tfrac{1}{n} * \sum (actual - forecast) \qquad (2)$$

n = number of items,
Σ = summation notation,
$Actual$ = original or observed y-value,
$Forecast$ = y-value from regression.

4.1.3   RMSE

It is more noticeable than MAE and lower RMSE value among various models to improve the presentation of that model shows in Eq. 3. R2 (Coefficient of assurance) Helps you to see how the free factor has changed with the flexibility of your model.

$$RMSE = \sqrt{\sum \frac{(Forecast - Actual)^2}{n}} \qquad (3)$$

To use the random tree regression, we used a number of scales like 1000 and the number of random circuits was 42. This measurement process is well suited for informal data where dependence between factors is difficult to identify. The Fig. 5 shows the proposed random forest method's performance matrix.

```
print('MAE:',metrics.mean_absolute_error(y_test,y_pred))
print('MSE:',metrics.mean_squared_error(y_test,y_pred))
print('RMSE:',np.sqrt(metrics.mean_squared_error(y_test,y_pred)))
[65]

... MAE: 1174.2753922793852
    MSE: 4360534.11473772
    RMSE: 2088.1891951491657
```

Fig. 5. Metrics of Random Forest algorithm

5   Conclusion and Future Scope

At the moment, there are a great deal of domains in which management is predicated on expectancies. One such domain is stock trading and management, which uses items that reflect the number of shares traded, such as Zestimate, which gives a proven quantity of the costs associated with real estate. In the airline industry, a need for management like this that can assist customers in booking tickets has arisen as a direct result of this need.

There has been a significant amount of study conducted on this topic making use of a variety of methods, and additional testing is anticipated to work towards understanding expectations through the use of a variety of statistics. Information that is more accurate and has better features can be used in the same way to get results that are more accurate.

In future, our research could be expanded to include air exchange ticketing data, which could provide additional insight into a specific schedule, such as time and date of departure, appearance, coverage, etc. Model weather forecast for daily flight or hourly rate. In addition, the cost of a flight on the market segment may be affected by the unpredictable influx of large numbers of travelers brought about by different events.

References

1. Sharma, L., Carpenter, M. (eds.): Analysis of machine learning techniques for airfare prediction. In: Computer Vision and Internet of Things: Technologies and Applications, 1st edn. Chapman and Hall/CRC (2022). https://doi.org/10.1201/9781003244165
2. Khandelwal, K., Sawarkar, A., Hira, S.: A novel approach for fare prediction using machine learning techniques. Int. J. Next Gener. Comput. Suppl. 12(5), 602–609 (2021). 8p.
3. Arjun, K.P., Achuthshankar, A., Soumya, M.K., Sreenarayanan, N.M., Priya, V.V., Faby, K.A.: PROvacy: protecting image privacy in social networking sites using reversible data hiding. In: 2016 10th International Conference on Intelligent Systems and Control (ISCO), pp. 1–4, January 2016
4. Gupta, J., Singh, I., Arjun, K.P.: Artificial Intelligence for Blockchain I, Blockchain, Internet of Things, and Artificial Intelligence, vol. 6. CRC Press, April 2021
5. Achuthshankar, A., Achuthshankar, A., Arjun, K., Sreenarayanan, N.: Encryption of reversible data hiding for better visibility and high security. Procedia Technol. 25, 216–223 (2016)
6. Groves, W., Gini, M.: An agent for optimizing airline ticket purchasing. In: Ito, Jonker, Gini, Shehory (eds.) Proceedings of the 12th International Conference on Autonomous Agents and Multiagent Systems (AAMAS 2013), Saint Paul, Minnesota, USA, 6–10 May 2013
7. Biswas, P., et al.: Flight price prediction: a case study. Int. J. Res. Appl. Sci. Eng. Technol. (IJRASET) 10(6) (2022). https://doi.org/10.22214/ijraset.2022.43666. ISSN: 2321-9653
8. Champawat, J.S., Arora, U., Vijaya, K.: Indian flight fare prediction: a proposal. Int. J. Adv. Technol. Eng. Sci. 9(3) (2021)
9. Tian, H., Presa-Reyes, M., Tao, Y., et al.: Data analytics for air travel data: a survey and new perspectives. ACM Comput. Surv. 54(8), 1–35 (2022)
10. Joseph, J., et al.: Flight ticket price predicting with the use of machine learning. Int. J. Adv. Trends Comput. Sci. Eng. 10(2), 1243–1246 (2021). https://doi.org/10.30534/IJATCSE/2021/1071022021
11. Oza, R.K., Jain, A.V., Raval, A.S.: Machine learning techniques for predicting airfare prices based on reviews 9(3) (2020). ISSN: 2319-8753 ISSN: 2347-6710
12. Tziridis, K., Kalampokas, T., Papakostas, G., Diamantaras, K.: Airfare price prediction using machine learning techniques. In: 25th European Signal Processing Conference (EUSIPCO) (2017)
13. Rajankar, S., Sakhrakar, N., Rajankar, O.: Flight fare prediction using machine learning algorithms. Int. J. Eng. Res. Technol. (IJERT) (2019)
14. Santos Domínguez-Menchero, J., Rivera, J., Torres-Manzanera, E.: Optimal purchase timing in the airline market. J. Air Transp. Manag. 40, 137–143 (2014). ISSN 0969-6997
15. Shabana, T., Afifa, S., Naziya, S., Mariya, K.: A novel machine learning methodology to increase sales in business services. Int. J. Comput. Sci. Eng. 6(12), 924–926 (2018)

16. Wang, T., et al.: A framework for airfare price prediction: a machine learning approach. In: 2019 IEEE 20th International Conference on Information Reuse and Integration for Data Science (IRI), pp. 200–207 (2019). https://doi.org/10.1109/IRI.2019.00041

17. Thirumuruganathan, S., Jung, S., Robillos, D.R., Salminen, J., Jansen, B.J.: Forecasting the nearly unforecastable: why aren't airline bookings adhering to the prediction algorithm? Electron. Commer. Res. **21**(1), 73–100 (2021)

18. Ratnakanth, G.: Prediction of flight fare using deep learning techniques. In: International Conference on Computing, Communication and Power Technology (IC3P), pp. 308–313 (2022). https://doi.org/10.1109/IC3P52835.2022.00071

19. Subramanian, R.R., Murali, M.S., Deepak, B., Deepak, P., Reddy, H.N., Sudharsan, R.R.: Airline fare prediction using machine learning algorithms. In: 2022 4th International Conference on Smart Systems and Inventive Technology (ICSSIT), pp. 877–884 (2022).: https://doi.org/10.1109/ICSSIT53264.2022.9716563

20. Abdella, J.A., Zaki, N., Shuaib, K., Khan, F.: Airline ticket price and demand prediction: a survey. J. King Saud Univ. Comput. Inf. Sci. **33**(4), 375–391 (2021)

Impact of Work from Home During Covid-19 on the Socio-economic Status of India

Poonam Ojha[1] (iD), Sudhanshu Maurya[2](✉) (iD), and Manish Kumar Ojha[3]

[1] School of Management, Graphic Era Hill University Bhimtal Campus, Nainital 263132, Uttarakhand, India
[2] School of Computing, Graphic Era Hill University Bhimtal Campus, Nainital, Uttarakhand 263132, India
dr.sm0302@gmail.com
[3] Amity University Noida, Noida, Uttar Pradesh, India

Abstract. Socioeconomic status (SES) is an instrument to measure the economic and social status of an individual or an economy concerning others. Though, Socioeconomic status is more commonly used to represent an economic difference in any society. Work from home is now a day (Covid-19) contributing to the nation for its socio-economic activities. This paper has examined the impact of 'work from home' on the socio-economic status of India as so many people became unemployed, the income of the society decreased as well as the Education system was worse affected. The present situation of the pestilence provided great importance to work from home (WFH) for many employees to have the opportunity to both carries on working and safely from the risk of virus vulnerability. As this Pandemic period is uncertain, working from home is more acceptable as the new normal working way. On the contrary, to find the impact of WFH on socioeconomic status, we took three variables: education, employment, and income & wealth.

Keywords: Work from home · Socio-economic status · Education · Income & wealth · Employment

1 Introduction

The socioeconomic study refers to the interaction between the social and economic behavior of a group of people, linking financial and social issues together. SES is a prominent indicator of any nation's economic as well as social position in the world. This index decides the togetherness of socio-economic activities. "Pandemics are not a new experience for the communities as they were recorded since prehistoric times. During each pandemic, major changes were noticed in the areas of economics, local and national policies, social behavior, and citizens' mentalities as well. Opposing these changes, it was detected that mentalities and social behavior were slightest potted as the institutionalized modifications [1], through public policies, were not adequately attached and synthesized with the psychosocial changes [2]." During the Pestilence of Covid-19, it is realized that SES has been affected severely because of aberration of

© The Author(s), under exclusive license to Springer Nature Switzerland AG 2022
R. Mehra et al. (Eds.): ICCISC 2022, CCIS 1672, pp. 100–113, 2022.
https://doi.org/10.1007/978-3-031-22915-2_9

social and economic activities. The COVID-19 pandemic is becoming furious and will have its long-term effects worldwide, most probably resulting in structural effects on the socio-economic status of India and other affected countries. "Like any other epidemics, COVID-19 has caused noteworthy changes on all levels of modern-day society [3–8]." The countrywide lockdown has ended up with financial losses as well as affected all segments of society including health, healthcare, and nutrition [15]. "Population density [9–11], high degree of mobility of humans, and mass socialization, as well as cultural, social, and tourism events [12–14] have been the basic reasons for COVID-19." In this description, in a nutshell, the main aim is to confer the effect of Work from Home in rejoinder to the pestilence on education, income & wealth, and employment in India.

1.1   Education

From preschool to tertiary education, the education system has been affected, resultantly worldwide policies have been introduced to target the complete shutdown of educational institutions. Consequently, UNESCO estimated that this shutdown procedure of educational facilities has affected almost 900 million learners. At the same time as the objective of these shutdowns is to prevent the spread of the virus and obviate carriage to defenseless individuals in the institutions, these shutdowns have had ubiquitous socioeconomic implications.

In the absence of a proper support system office, work, and household work, as well as home time and school time, were inseparable during the lockdown and the playtime for children became zero [16]. "Every house became a school and each parent a teacher, during lockdown when schools and colleges were closed across India. There was no boundary between the playtime and my time for millions of children in the country. Further, it was realized the paucity of a structured learning environment at home with having a worse impact on overall learning and consequently affected the overall education outcome [16]", education and SES are depicted in Fig. 1.

"As almost 70% of the 1.4 million schools and 51,000 colleges with nearly 300 million children are run by government bodies in India, the rural schools and the parents now face a bleak education system and emptiness even as government's advisories ask schools to go online, and the government is looking at ways in which course can be designed so students do not suffer." The impact of a long-term school shutdown is yet to be seen.

1.2   Employment

Many IT sector companies prefer WFH at a wide scale to enhance workplace flexibility [17] and to reduce the worst impact on Society. The sudden importance and growth of WFH have increased investigation of the WFH phenomenon, especially intending to identify the number of jobs that can be done casually [18–22]. In general, the literature overlooks the possible effects of WFH along with the unequal distribution of wages and income. The causes of inequalities are multiple and distinct and have been growing in eminence in policymakers, employment, and SES are depicted in Fig. 2.

According to Pouliakas and Branka (2020) and Fana et al. (2020), "the most defense-less groups, such as women, non-natives, those with non-standard contracts (self-employed and temporary workers), the lower educated, those employed in micro-sized workplaces, and low-wage workers has been impacted by the COVID-19 pandemic." Consequently, Palomino et al. (2020) in their findings find that the crisis has increased the levels of inequality and poverty [23]. Beland et al. (2020) examined "the short-term consequences of COVID-19 on employment and wages as in his findings suggested that the unemployment rate has been increased due to COVID-19; Working Hours and labor force participation has decreased and had no significant impacts on wages [23]." Also, this crisis has increased labor market inequalities. "According to the World Economic Forum, the current pestilence compelled migrants to be trapped abroad and compromise to the unfavorable circumstances, by taking up low-wage jobs, living in poor working conditions, restricting spending, and thus, risk exposure to infections like the coronavirus [24]."

1.3 Income and Wealth

Under our best observation, this study first shows how an increase in WFH would have an impact on changes in income and wealth, as shown in Fig. 3. The lower socio-economic stratum (SES) has been greatly affected by the economic downturn during the current pandemic [15]. "The three main areas that have an economic impact of covid-19 are given below:

- Elevation in poverty i.e., approaching more people below the poverty line [25]
- Aggravation of socio-economic disparities [26, 27], and
- Conciliation in health-related precautions (use of masks, social distancing, looking for medical guidance in case of cough and fever, etc.)."

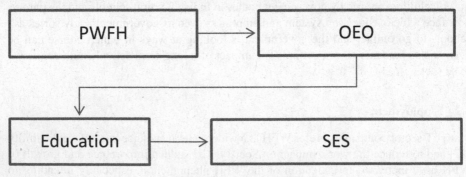

Fig. 1. Education and SES

In the current situation inequalities of income & wealth shocked younger households and middle-aged households respectively. One of the disruptions which are caused by this pandemic has had a major bang on the remittance flows used by migrant Indian

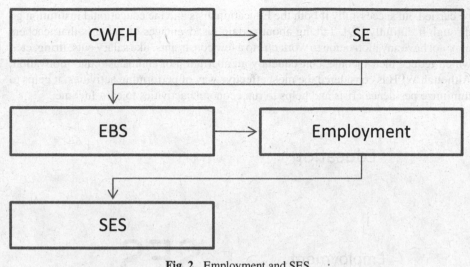

Fig. 2. Employment and SES

workers; works as one of the ways of poverty diminution, economic development, and boosting GDP. In India, remittances are anticipated to go down by about 23% in 2020; with a remarkable gap to a growth of 5.5% in 2019 [28]. WFH system has emerged with Covid-19, under which the people were suggested to work, study, and worship from home.

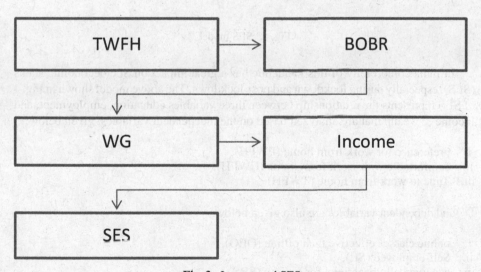

Fig. 3. Income and SES

Educationalists were also invited to adopt work from home system using technology, as per the orders of The Ministry of Education. WFH for teachers has a few advantages and disadvantages as well, for the performance of teachers. Also Work from home can be carried out successfully if both the Educationalists and the educational institution go through it dutifully [29]. Talking about certain disadvantages of WFH is that teachers may not have any motivation to work due to a few constraints, like salary cuts, firing, etc., which reduce their income, consequently an aberration of enthusiasm and motivation. Although WFH is considered the most effective way of performing activities, it helps to minimize pestilence crisis and helps to run economic activities to earn Income.

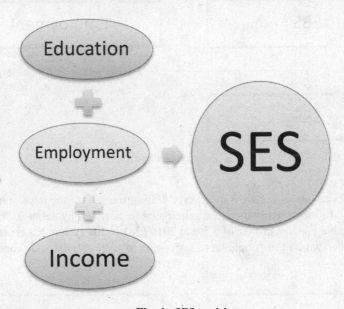

Fig. 4. SES model

In India comorbidity of this Pandemic has a great impact on Socioeconomic status (SES), especially during lockdown and post-lockdown. The above model shown in Fig. 4 of SES represents the relationship between three variables education, employment, and Income & wealth that are analyzed based on the independent variables, given below:

i.   preference for work from home (PWFH),
ii.   comfortable with work from home (CWFH),
iii. Time to work from home (TWFH)

and dependent variables are also given below:

i.   online classes effective than offline (OEO),
ii.   Self-employed (SE),
iii. economically beneficial for society (EBS)
iv.   boost in online business revenue (BOBR) and
v.   larger wealth gap (WG).

One of the most notable to this model is the socio-economic status of India is framed by OEO, SE, EBS, BOBR, and the WG. During covid-19, the online classes were more effective than Offline classes as children realized as per their safety basis with this the online business revenue has increased as various activities have only one way to be performed i.e., Online. People enjoyed lockdown with the help of online games and other entertainment options, hence we can say lockdown enhanced the use of online platforms. Due to this pandemic, people realized to have technical knowledge that again encouraged cognitive behavior. Revenue from online businesses encouraged online employment in the form of self-employment which could decrease unemployment. WFH also has optimistic brim over effects on workers as it is beneficial to them for increased income and reduced infection risks [18].

"As in the US economy [23], Beland et al. (2020) examined that covid-19 leads to an increase in the unemployment rate, working hours, as well as the participation of the labor force, has decreased; India faced the same issues due to which income and employment level went down." This happening allows other problems, like a larger wealth gap with increased income inequalities and poverty to have emerged. Further, this increased the scope for self-employment during the post-lockdown period under a good preview of the SES (Socio-economic status) of India. For the growth of any economy like India, SE & BOBR play a vital role to design a dignified SES. With this reference model of SES, we examined the performance of the OEO, SE, BOBR & wealth gap in the landscape of education, employment, and income & wealth to encourage the growth of SES in India. Pandemic is responsible for shutting down certain employment opportunities, decreased income sources, and more impact on education, but on the contrary, we found certain development in these fields. Likewise, innovations are positively related to worse conditions, as it is said in a worse situation when we have no more options, the human mind conquers new ideas, and it leads to innovations. With these arguments, we analyzed that SES is the outcome of alterations we have in OEO, SE, EBS, BOBR, and WG as these were enhanced during this crisis.

2 Theoretical Background and Hypothesis Development

In this paper, we took 257 respondents from schools, Universities, professionals, industry persons, and academicians from corner to corner via social media platform (WhatsApp) in India to understand the effect of WFH on education, employment, and Income in India. The data is limited to a few states like Uttar Pradesh, New Delhi, Uttarakhand, Maharashtra, Gujarat, Punjab, Assam, Bihar, and West Bengal. Drawn from our arguments and past research we developed three hypotheses. Under the surveillance of covid-19; the study was conducted based on primary data collection (n = 257) in online mode. We selected University students, teachers, and other participants on a convenience sampling basis to ensure feasibility. Quite a lot of advantages and disadvantages to the WFH program have been observed by different researchers, as WFH activity is more flexible than the physical activities to complete the work [29]. In education as well as in other professions like IT sectors the stress level has been decreased with a distancing from traffic jams and also have more free time for family. This gives a boost for the employees to strengthen their ability.

Various research has confirmed that WFH is beneficial for the health of the country socially and economically [30], hence we thought to go for an analysis of the Impact of

WFH on the SES of any nation, like India. For this, we tried to get information related to the three elements of SES (education, health, and income) that define the health of any nation.

We had a set of questions through an online survey anonymously, using the non-probability snowball sampling technique that has been framed first on demographics like age and gender; then the questions were divided into three parts

i.   Education
ii.   Employment
iii. Income & wealth.

For the first part of the questionnaire, we asked teachers & professors, do they feel comfortable with online classes? and do these online classes are more effective than offline? Further, the questionnaire consists of two questions that have been asked to private employees (teachers & professors, low and middle-class workers, and Industry persons) do they think work from home is economically beneficial for society? and Do self-employment is the outcome of 'work from home' during this pandemic? Finally, we asked three questions to them including estate dealers and purchasers; do they think it is appropriate or suitable for the health of any nation? Do online movements facilitate a boost in revenue from online businesses? do Wealth gaps (like income equality) become larger during this Pandemic?

H1: Effect of WFH on Education regarding the independent variable PWFH and dependent variable OEO.
H2: Impact of WFH on Employment regarding the Independent variable CWFH and dependent variables SE and EBS.
H3: Impact of WFH on Income& wealth regarding the independent variable TWFH and dependent variables BOBR and WG.
H4: SES depends on PWFH, CWFH, and TWFH with the special reference to education, employment, and income & wealth.

The collected information was then analyzed by Simple Linear Regression analysis in SPSS. We examined close relationships between different variables taken in the study. Based on Descriptive Statistics, we found the Range = 1, mean (n = 257) =1.44, S.D. = 0.499 of all respondents.

A. Study 1: We took 100 students and teachers out of 257 respondents and found that online study is more effective than offline as it reduces infection risks and enhanced the technical knowledge of both. Further, the results i.e., $P < 0.002$, $R2 = 0.131$, and $F = 10.266$ stated that the overall regression model was significant. This has suggested that students and teachers prefer online classes, consequently preferring WFH and so contributing to the growth of SES, as shown in Tables 1, 2, and 3.

Table 1. Model summary

Model	R	R square	Adjusted R square	Std. error of the estimate
1	.360[a]	.131	.118	.939

[a]Predictors: (Constant), PWFH.

$R^2 = 0.131$; taken as a set, the predictors i.e., dependent variables account for 13.1% of the variance in the independent variable.

Table 2. ANOVA[a](test using alpha $= 0.05$)

Model		Sum of squares	Df	Mean square	F	Sig.
1	Regression	9.052	1	9.052	10.266	.002[b]
	Residual	60.836	69	.882		
	Total	69.887	70			

[a]Dependent Variable: OEO.
[b]Predictors: (Constant), PWFH.
The overall regression model was significant, F = (9.052, 60.836) = **10.266,**

Table 3. Co-efficients[a] (test each predictor at alpha $= 0.05$)

Model		Unstandardized coefficients		Standardized coefficients	t	Sig.
		B	Std. error	Beta		
1	(Constant)	2.861	.274		10.457	.000
	PWFH	.376	.118	.360	3.204	.002

[a]Dependent Variable: OEO.

B. *Study 2:* This study deals with the second hypothesis, where we found that EBS is insignificant at $P < 0.221$, $R^2 = 0.023$, but SE is significant with $P < 0.001$, $R^2 = 0.157$. Examining this we can state that self-employment has been encouraged during Covid-19, on the contrary, WFH is not economically beneficial for society because of a dearth of motivation, and competition and has hampered Industrial work (fieldwork), as shown in Tables 4, 5, and 6.

During this pestilence, self-employment has been encouraged due to less employment in the economy and cutting of salaries, which discouraged employees to remain in the job. Although the business also had many constraints during this period, still people were ready to engage themselves in business activities.

C. *Study 3:* An extrapolation of the below preliminary findings suggests that the first variable in TWFH is 'boost in online business revenue' has no significant effect on SES. From the results, we found $P < 0.725$, $R^2 = 0.002$ which shows only 0.2% of the variance

Table 4. Model summary

Model	R	R square	Adjusted R square	Std. error of the estimate
1	.147[a]	.023	.008	1.071

[a]Predictors: (Constant), CWFH.

$R^2 = .023$; taken as a set, the predictors i.e., dependent variables account for 2.3% of the variance in the independent variable.

Table 5. ANOVA[a] (test using alpha = 0.05)

Model		Sum of squares	Df	Mean square	F	Sig.
1	Regression	1.755	1	1.755	1.528	.221[b]
	Residual	79.203	69	1.148		
	Total	80.958	70			

[a]Dependent Variable: EBS.
[b]Predictors: (Constant), CWFH.

The overall regression model was significant, F = (1.755, 79.203) = 1.528.

Table 6. Coefficients[a] (test each predictor at alpha = 0.05)

Model		Unstandardized coefficients		Standardized coefficients	t	Sig.
		B	Std. error	Beta		
1	(Constant)	2.090	.277		7.548	.000
	CWFH	.132	.107	.147	1.236	.221

[a]Dependent Variable: EBS.

in the independent variable. Although during lockdown people at home preferred to play online and also it has been observed predilection for online entertainment, as shown in Tables 7, 8, And 9.

Table 7. Model summary

Model	R	R square	Adjusted R square	Std. error of the estimate
1	.396[a]	.157	.145	1.071

[a.]Predictors: (Constant), CWFH.

$R^2 = 0.157$; taken as a set, the predictors i.e., dependent variables account for 15.7% of the variance in the independent variable

Table 8. ANOVA[a] (test using alpha = 0.05)

Model		Sum of squares	Df	Mean square	F	Sig.
1	Regression	14.740	1	14.740	12.842	.001[b]
	Residual	79.203	69	1.148		
	Total	93.944	70			

[a]Dependent Variable: SE.
[b]Predictors: (Constant), CWFH.

Table 9. Coefficients (test each predictor at alpha = 0.05)

Model		Unstandardized coefficients		Standardized coefficients	t	Sig.
		B	Std. error	Beta		
1	(Constant)	1.090	.277		3.937	.000
	CWFH	.382	.107	.396	3.584	.001

[a]Dependent Variable: SE.
The overall regression model was significant, F = (14.740, 79.203) = **12.842.**

D. Study 4: In this study, we examined the relationship between TWFH and WG to know whether these variables are interconnected or not. Although we know that there is a very close relationship but during the pandemic, income decreased at a remarkable rate and for this reason, our analysis showed insignificant results and a low percentage of variance. People need more time for WFH and the income to be increased; it is predicted that WFH is preferred by It companies and others forever, in that case, Income will increase and SES as well. R2 = 0.005; taken as a set, the predictors i.e., dependent variables account for0.5% of the variance in the independent variable, shown in Tables 10, 11, 12, 13, 14, and 15.

Table 10. Model summary

Model	R	R square	Adjusted R square	Std. error of the estimate
1	.043[a]	.002	−.013	.855

[a]Predictors: (Constant), TWFH.
R^2 = 0.002, taken as a set, the predictors i.e., dependent variables account for 0.2% of the variance in the independent variable

The above analysis revealed that WG and BOBR have insignificant relations, but both have a positive relationship with SES. Shreds of evidence from Tables 4 and 5 explain the reason why WFH was one of the instruments in reducing infection rates during the early days of the pestilence.

Table 11. ANOVA[a] (test using alpha = 0.05)

Model		Sum of squares	Df	Mean square	F	Sig.
1	Regression	.091	1	.091	.125	.725[b]
	Residual	50.387	69	.730		
	Total	50.479	70			

[a]Dependent Variable: BOBR.
[b]Predictors: (Constant), TWFH.
The overall regression model was significant, F = (0.091, 50.387) = **12.842.**

Table 12. Coefficients[a] (test each predictor at alpha = 0.05)

Model		Unstandardized coefficients		Standardized coefficients	t	Sig.
		B	Std. error	Beta		
1	(Constant)	1.541	.281		5.478	.000
	TWFH	.034	.097	.043	.354	.725

[a]Dependent Variable: BOBR.

Table 13. Model summary

Model	R	R square	Adjusted R square	Std. error of the estimate
1	.071[a]	.007	−.010	1.236

[a]Predictors: (Constant), TWFH.

Table 14. ANOVA[a] (test using alpha = 0.05)

Model		Sum of squares	Df	Mean square	F	Sig
1	Regression	.515	1	.515	.337	.563[b]
	Residual	105.401	69	1.528		
	Total	105.915	70			

[a]Dependent Variable: WG.
[b]Predictors: (Constant), TWFH.
The overall regression model was significant, F = (0.515, 105.401) = **0 .337.**

3   Conclusion

During the period of pestilence, we all are moving with a threat of being caught in this trap of pandemic and don't have any clues on how to get rid of the situation; we are worried for our family and obviously for us too, knowing the adverse impact of

Table 15. Coefficients[a] (test each predictor at alpha = 0.05)

Model		Unstandardized coefficients		Standardized coefficients	t	Sig.
		B	Std. error	Beta		
1	(Constant)	2.047	.407		5.032	.000
	TWFH	.081	.140	.070	.581	.563

[a]Dependent Variable: WG.

covid-19. For the time being, we have vaccination now, but every higher authority has question marks in their minds about whether they can solve this issue at that level of desire of the public. Many efforts have been done to fight with covid-19, but not got the final solution. In between that, every nation tried to overcome this issue at its best levels. India also revealed the best part of its socio-economic aspects by balancing the situation by applying WFH which is the utmost during the pandemic. This paper argued that work from home is very much effective as it saves lives and the economy as well. All else equal, the education, employment and income level of the economy have a worse impact because of this pandemic and WFH allows reducing infection risk while maintaining both economic and social activities. In this paper we took these (education, employment, and income)three parts of SES as indicators and compared them with a preference for work from home (PWFH), comfortable with work from home (CWFH), & Time to work from home (TWFH) as independent variables; and dependent variables i) online classes effective than offline (OEO), ii) Self-employed (SE), iii) economically beneficial for society (EBS) iv) boost in online business revenue (BOBR) and v) larger wealth gap(WG); to examine the relationships. The results were shocking for different dependent variables, we found the significant relations of all to SES except one variable i.e., WG which gave insignificant results during the first phase of covid-19. We examined that WFH benefited the socio-economic part of the nation with few negative impacts that imply WFH should be encouraged as long as noteworthy virus risk remains.

References

1. Sonia, S.: Pandemic: Tracking Contagions, From Cholera to Ebola and Beyond. Sarah Crichton Books, New York (2016). ISBN 978-0-374-12288-1
2. Saini, S.: COVID-19 may double poverty in India [Internet] Financial Express 2020. https://www.financialexpress.com/opinion/covid-19-may-double-poverty-in-india/194 3736/. Accessed 22 May 2020
3. Purwanto, A., et al.: Impact of work from home (WFH) on Indonesian teachers performance during the Covid-19 pandemic: an exploratory study. Int. J. Adv. Sci. Technol. **29**(5), 6235–6244 (2020)
4. Bick, A., Blandin, A., Mertens, K.: Work from home after the Covid-19 outbreak. CEPR Discussion Paper No. DP15000
5. Alon, T., Doepke, M., Rumsey, J.-O., Tertilt, M.: The impact of COVID-19 on gender equality. In: NBERvWorking Papers 26947. Inc, National Bureau of Economic Research (2020)

6. Anser, M.K., Yousaf, Z., Khan, M.A., Nassani, A.A., Alotaibi, S.M., Qazi Abro, M.M., et al.: Does communicable diseases (including COVID-19) may increase global poverty risk? A cloud on the horizon. Environ. Res. **15**(187), 109668 (2020)

7. Atkeson, A.: What will be the Economic Impact of COVID-19 in the US? Rough Estimates of Disease Scenarios. National Bureau of Economic Research, Cambridge (2020). http://www.nber.org/Papers/w26867. Accessed 21 June 2020

8. Baker, S., Bloom, N., Davis, S., Kost, K., Sammon, M., Viratyosin, T.: The Unprecedented Stock Market Impact of COVID-19. https://www.nber.org/papers/w26945. Accessed May 21 2020

9. Bartik, A., Bertrand, M., Cullen, Z., Glaeser, E., Luca, M., Stanton, C.: How Are Small Businesses Adjusting to COVID19? Early Evidence from a Survey. National Bureau of Economic Research, Cambridge (2020). https://www.nber.org/papers/w26989. Accessed 21 June 2020

10. Béland, L.-P., Brodeur, A., Wright, T.: The short-term economic consequences of COVID-19: exposure to disease, remote work and government response. IZA Discussion Paper Series (13159) (2020)

11. Di Gennaro, F., et al.: Coronavirus diseases (COVID-19) current status and future perspectives: a narrative review. Int. J. Environ. Res. Public Health **17**, 2690 (2020).

12. Dingel, J., Neiman, B.: How many jobs can be done at home? National Bureau of Economic Research No. 26948 (2020)

13. Guerrieri, V., Lorenzoni, G., Straub, L., Werning, I.: Macroeconomic Implications of COVID-19: Can Negative Supply Shocks Cause Demand Shortages? National Bureau of Economic Research, Cambridge (2020). http://www.nber.org/papers/w26918.pdf. Accessed 21 June 2020

14. Guermond, V., Datta, K.: How coronavirus could hit the billions migrant workers send home [Internet] World Economic Forum 2020. https://www.weforum.org/agenda/2020/04/how-coronavirus-could-hitthe-Billions-migrant-workers-send-home/. Accessed 23 Apr 2020

15. Mccloskey, B., et al.: Mass gathering events and reducing further global spread of COVID-19: a political and publicHealth dilemma. Lancet **395**, 1096–1099 (2020)

16. Bonacini, L., Gallo, G., Scicchitano, S.: Working from home and income inequality: risks of a 'new normal' with COVID-19. J. Popul. Econ. **34**, 303–360 (2021)

17. Mahendradev, S.: Addressing COVID-19 impacts on agriculture, food security, and livelihoods in India | IFPRI: international food policy research institute. IFPRI. https://www.ifpri.org/Blog/addressing-covid-19-impacts-agriculture-food-security-and-livelihoods-India. Accessed 22 May 2020

18. Alipour, J.V., Fadinger, H., Schymik, J.: My home is my castle – the benefits of working from home during a pandemic crisis. J. Public Econ. **196**, 104373 (2021)

19. Kang, D., Choi, H., Kim, J.H., Choi, J.: Spatial epidemic dynamics of the COVID-19 outbreak in China. Int. J. Infect. Dis. **94**, 96–102 (2020)

20. Koren, M., Peto, R.: Business disruptions from social distancing. In: Covid Economics (2), 13–31. Press, CEPRIZA Discussion Paper No. 1328133 Pages Posted, 23 May 2020 Konstantinos Pouliakas Cedefop, University of Aberdeen - Business School, IZA Institute of Labor Economics Jiri Branka (2020)

21. Leibovici, F., Santacrue, A.M., Famiglietti, M.: Social distancing and contact-intensive occupations. St. Louis Federal Reserve Bank - On the Economy Blog, March (2020)

22. Lemay, M.C.: Global Pandemic Threats: A Reference Handbook. ABC-CLIO, Santa Barbara (2020). ISBN 978-1-4408-4282-5

23. Honigsbaum, M.: The Pandemic Century: One Hundred Years of Panic, Hysteria, and Hubris. W. W. Norton & Company, New York (2019). ISBN 978-0393254754

24. Ito, H., Hanaoka, S., Kawasaki, T.: The cruise industry and the COVID-19 outbreak. Transp. Res. Interdiscip. Perspect. **5**, 100136 (2020)

25. Mongey, S., Pilossoph, L., Weinberg. A.: Which workers bear the burden of social distancing policies? NBER Working Paper No. 27085 (2020)

26. Fana, M., Torrejon Prez, S., Fernandez-Macias, E.: Employment impact of Covid-19: from short term effects to long terms prospects. J. Ind. Bus. Econ. **47**, 391–410 (2020)

27. Pouliakas, K., Branka, J.: EU Jobs at highest risk of Covid-19 social distancing: will the pandemic exacerbate labour market divide? IZA discussion paper no. 13281. https://ssrn.com/abstract=3608530

28. Praharaj, S., Vaidya, H.: The Urban Dimension of COVID-19 in India: COVID Outbreak and Lessons for Future Cities. https://www.researchgate.net/publication/341616744_The_urban_dimension_of_COVID19_in_India_COVID_Outbreak_and_Lessons_for_Future_Cities?Channel=doi&Linkid=5ecb837492851c11a8880043&showfulltext=true. Accessed 21 May 2020

29. Prashant, K.N., Khanna, P.: Every house a school, every parent a teacher as Covid-19 impacts education of 300mn students. https://www.livemint.com/news/india/every-house-a-school-every-parent-a-teacher-as-covid-19-impacts-education-11585140662556.html

30. Adams-Prassl, A., Boneva, T., Golin, M., Rauh, C.: Inequality in the impact of the coronavirus shock: evidence from real-time surveys. IZA Discussion Paper No. 13183 (2020)

Author Index

Printed in the United States
by Baker & Taylor Publisher Services

Printed in the United States
by Baker & Taylor Publisher Services